Beginning Sous Vide

Low Temperature
Recipes and Techniques
for Getting Started at Home

By Jason Logsdon

Presented By CookingSousVide.com

Table of Contents

Intro to Sous Vide

Sous vide is quickly becoming one of the hottest new culinary techniques. Here are the ins and outs you need to know to get started.

If you have any questions you can ask them in the "How-Tos" section on our website. Just post your question and other sous vide cooks will weigh in with their answers.

You can find it on our website at:
www.cookingsousvide.com/how-to

History of Sous Vide

Sous vide, or low temperature cooking, is the process of cooking food at a very tightly controlled temperature, normally the temperature the food will be served at. This is a departure from traditional cooking methods that use high heat to cook the food, which must be removed at the exact moment it reaches the desired temperature.

Sous vide was first used as an upscale culinary technique in kitchens in France in the 1970s and traditionally is the process of cooking vacuum sealed food in a low temperature water bath. This process helps to achieve texture and doneness not found in other cooking techniques, as well as introducing many conveniences for a professional kitchen. Sous Vide has slowly been spreading around the world in professional kitchens everywhere and is finally making the jump to home kitchens.

As sous vide has become more popular and moved to the home kitchen the term now encompasses both traditional "under vacuum" sous vide and also low temperature cooking. Some preparations rely on the vacuum pressure to change the texture of the food but in most cases the benefits of sous vide are realized in the controlled, low temperature cooking process. This means that fancy vacuum sealers can be set aside for home sealers or even ziploc bags.

How it Works

The basic concept of sous vide cooking is that food should be cooked at the temperature it will be served at. For instance, if you are cooking a steak to medium rare, you want to serve it at 131°F.

With traditional cooking methods you would normally cook it on a hot grill or oven at around 400°F-500°F and pull it off at the right moment when the middle has reached 131°F. This results in a bulls eye effect of burnt meat on the outside turning to medium rare in the middle. This steak cooked sous vide would be cooked at 131°F for several hours. This will result in the entire piece of meat being a perfectly cooked medium rare. The steak would then usually be quickly seared at high heat to add the flavorful, browned crust to it.

There are two basic components to sous vide cooking at home: temperature and time. Each one of these can affect the end quality, texture, and taste of sous vide dishes. Learning to understand how they affect the food is one of the most important things as you begin sous vide cooking.

Temperature

All sous vide cooking is done at temperatures below the boiling point of water and normally not above 185°F. You usually cook the food at the temperature you want it served at, so most settings are between 120°F and 185°F, depending on the food being prepared.

While the range of temperature used in sous vide is much less variable than for traditional cooking, the precise control of the temperature is of great importance. When you set your oven at 400°F it actually fluctuates about 50 degrees, sending it between 375°F and 425°F, which is fine when cooking at high temperatures. When cooking sous vide, the temperature of the water determines the doneness of your food, so a 50°F fluctuation would result in over cooked food. Most sous vide machines fluctuate less than 1°F and the best are less than 0.1°F.

This precision is why many sous vide machines are very expensive. However, there are many more home machines available in the last few years, some good do-it-yourself kits, and even some ways to accomplish "accurate enough" sous vide on the cheap. We will discuss many of your options in our *Sous Vide Equipment* chapter.

Time

Cooking tenderizes food by breaking down its internal structure. This process happens faster at higher temperatures. Because sous vide is done at such low temperatures the cooking time needs to be increased to achieve the same tenderization as traditional techniques.

Also, your window of time to perfectly cooked food is much longer than with traditional cooking methods because you are cooking the food at the temperature you want it to end up at, rather than a higher temperature. This also allows you to leave food in the water bath even after it is done since keeping it at this temperature does not dry out the food, up to several hours longer for tougher cuts of meat. However, be careful not to take this concept too far as food can still become overcooked by sous vide, many times without showing it externally.

Temperature and Time Together

The power of sous vide cooking comes from precisely controlling both temperature and time. This is important because of the way meat reacts to different temperatures.

At 120°F meat slowly begins to tenderize as the protein myosin begins to coagulate and the connective tissue in the meat begins to break down. As the temperature increases so does the speed of tenderization.

However, meat also begins to lose its moisture above 140°F as the heat causes the collagen in the cells to shrink and wring out the moisture. This happens very quickly over 150°F and meat becomes completely dried out above 160°F.

Many tough cuts of meat are braised or roasted for a long period of time so the meat can fully tenderize, but because of the high temperatures they can easily become dried out. Using sous vide allows you to hold the meat below the 140°F barrier long enough for the slower tenderization process to be effective. This results in very tender meat that is still moist and not overcooked.[1]

Benefits of Sous Vide

Just like any method of cooking there are many reasons to use the sous vide technique, depending on what you are trying to accomplish.

Moisture

Because food cooked in the sous vide style is sealed it does not lose moisture or flavor to the cooking medium. The sous vide pouch holds in all the liquid released by the food. This is especially apparent when compared to traditional techniques such as roasting and braising where the meat has a tendency to dry out.

Also, as discussed in the *Temperature and Time Together* section, the low heat used in sous vide prevents the collagen from constricting and forcing out more moisture. Controlling the collagen combined with the vacuum sealing results in very moist foods.

Tenderness

The sous vide technique allows you to cook tough cuts of meat at an incredibly low temperature, allowing you to tenderize them while remaining perfectly medium-rare. This is very effective for shanks, roasts and other pieces of meat that are typically braised or roasted, but often dry out or get overcooked in the process.

Texture

Using sous vide to cook food also exposes new textures. This is caused by two things. First, the vacuum sealing process can make lighter foods denser, like watermelon. Second, the lack of high heat used in cooking can result in silky and smoothly textured food that is impossible to replicate with traditional cooking techniques.

Convenience

Sous vide introduces many time saving and general convenience strategies for the home cook. We discuss several in more detail in the *Tips and Tricks* section ranging from "Beer Cooler Sous Vide" to hassle-free freezer steaks.

Disadvantages of Sous Vide

Like any culinary technique, sous vide cooking also has its drawbacks. Fortunately, the first two are slowly disappearing as sous vide becomes a more prevalent technique and the affect of the third can be minimized with planning.

Information

Even though the amount of information about sous vide has increased a lot over the past few years it can still be hard to find specific information. While there is information out there on websites, forums, books, and magazines, there often isn't a single repository you can use to collect it. This has meant a lot of time lost on research before even getting started.

This book will be enough to get you familiarized with sous vide and started on many recipes. It will also direct you where to find more information as you become more experienced with the technique.

High Cost

The second disadvantage is the high cost of good sous vide equipment. Until recently, the only effective way to do sous vide cooking was by using thermal immersion circulators or thermal circulating water baths, both of which run more than a thousand dollars.

Now, some less-expensive alternatives are turning up, such as sous vide cooking controllers, that reduce the cost of getting started to a few hundred dollars. In the last year there have also been several high quality devices released specifically for the home chef that offer very good temperature control.

This book covers many different options for getting started in the *Sous Vide Equipment* chapter.

Time

The third potential disadvantage is the length of time required to cook some items with sous vide. Even more than braising or roasting, most sous vide cooking requires long periods of time. For many tougher cuts of meat, such as short ribs or brisket, it is recommended you cook them at about 130°F for around 36 hours. Of course, the majority of this time you don't have to do a single thing to them and the energy expended is minimal. There are also several types of sous vide cooking that can be done in 30 to 60 minutes, especially for fish and chicken dishes.

Hype

Since sous vide is currently a hip technique many people talk about how it is the future of cooking. While sous vide can do many extraordinary things it will never replace traditional techniques, any more than the oven replaced grilling.

Many people try to capitalize on the popularity of sous vide by trotting out various un-inspired preparations. Just be aware that like any cooking technique sous vide can be done poorly, especially when applied to the wrong dishes, or by a skilled chef it can be done exquisitely.

Anytime you approach a dish you should think about what is the best technique to use, and sous vide will not always be the answer.

Basic Sous Vide Technique

At the heart of sous vide cooking is a very simple process. While there are variations within each dish, almost every sous vide meal follows the same steps.

Flavor the Food

Just like many traditional methods, you often times flavor the food before cooking it. This can be as simple as a sprinkling of salt and pepper or as complicated as adding an elaborate sauce, spice rub, or even smoking the food. Depending on the type of seasoning it can either be rubbed directly onto the food itself or added into the pouch with the food.

If you are using a normal home vacuum sealer and want to add more than a little liquid, freeze the liquid before adding it to the pouch. This way the process of vacuum sealing will not suck out the liquid. Otherwise, you can normally use food grade ziploc bags to seal food with liquids.

In our various food sections we give some tips and suggested recipes for flavoring your food. But remember, just like traditional cooking a lot of the fun comes with experimenting.

Seal the Food

Once the seasoning and food have been added to the pouch, remove the air and seal it closed. Removing the air results in closer contact between the food and the water in the water bath. This helps to facilitate quicker cooking since water transfers heat more efficiently than air.

Sealing the food can be done with anything from ziplocs or food grade plastic wrap to a FoodSaver Vacuum Sealer or even a chambered vacuum sealer.

Some vacuum sealers have different strengths of vacuum to seal the bag and can be used to affect the texture of some types of food.

Various vacuum sealing options are discussed in the *Vacuum Sealers* section of the *Sous Vide Equipment* chapter.

Heat the Water

Simply bring the water bath up to the temperature you will cook at. This water bath will normally be the same temperature that you will want your food to end up at.

Depending on the type of heat regulator, you may be able to have the food in the water while it heats. For others, it is best to preheat the water before placing the food in it due to early fluctuations in temperature.

The *Temperature Regulation* section of the *Sous Vide Equipment* chapter discusses the various temperature regulators and water baths available from a pot on the stove to a professional immersion circulator.

Cook the Food

Put the food pouch in the water and let it cook for the amount of time specified in the recipe or on the Time and Temperature chart. For items that are cooked for longer amounts of time it can be good to rotate the food every 6 to 10 hours, especially if you are using less precise sous vide equipment.

At some higher temperatures the sous vide pouches can float due to air released from the food. If that happens you might have to use a plate or bowl to weigh them down.

Finish the Dish

To get a good finish and texture to your food, especially meats, many times it is advisable to quickly sear the meat in a saute pan or with a blow torch. Some meals also call for other methods of finishing the food, such as breading and deep-frying for chicken or mashing potatoes with cream and butter for mashed potatoes.

You can also quickly chill the food in an ice bath and then refrigerate or freeze the food for later re-heating.

Sous Vide Safety

Safety is always a concern with any cooking method. Here are the basics you need to understand so you can begin to see how sous vide and food safety interact.

Sous vide is a new and largely untested method of cooking. It potentially carries many inherent health risks that may not be fully understood. We have done our best to provide the latest information and what is currently understood about this form of cooking.

However, we feel that anyone undertaking sous vide cooking, or any other method of cooking, should fully inform themselves about any and all risks associated with it and come to their own conclusions about its safety. Following anything in this book may make you or your guests sick and should only be done if you are fully aware of the potential risks and complications.

There are two main concerns when it comes to sous vide cooking, they are pathogens and the dangers of cooking in plastic.

Pathogens, Bacteria and Salmonella

One large safety concern with sous vide that has been studied in great detail deals with the propagation of bacteria at various temperatures, especially salmonella. Salmonella only thrive in a certain range of temperatures, from about 40°F to 130°F, often referred to as the "danger zone".

This danger zone is why we refrigerate our foods until an hour or so before we are ready to cook them. It is also why we cook our foods to specific temperatures before we eat them.

The biggest misconception about bacteria and the danger zone is that any food in the temperature range is not safe and as soon as you move above 130°F the food instantly

becomes safe. The truth is that the bacteria begin to die in direct relation to the temperature they are exposed to.

The best way to visualize this is to think about how we humans react to heat. We do fine in climates where the temperature is below 100°F. However, once it begins to climb around 110°F or 120°F you begin to hear about deaths in the news due to heat stroke. If the temperature were to raise to 200°F stepping outside for more than a few seconds would kill you.

Bacteria behave in the exact same way. They begin to die at around 130°F to 135°F and 165°F just about instantly kills them. You can see this in the chart below, based on the USDA data[2] replicated in the *Required Cooking Time* section. At 136°F it takes about 63 minutes for your food to be safe and at 146°F it only takes 7 minutes to become safe.

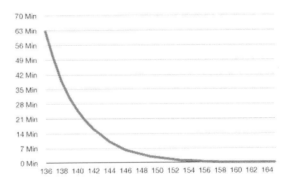

This concept is why the USDA recommends that chicken is cooked to 165°F, because at that temperature it takes only a few seconds for enough bacteria to die to achieve acceptable safety levels. In comparison, at 136°F it takes 63.3 minutes at that temperature to achieve the same safety level, something that is virtually impossible using traditional cooking methods. Using sous vide makes it possible to heat chicken and other meats to an internal temperature of as low as 130°F and hold it there long enough to kill the bacteria.

Please remember that this is assuming that your thermometer is exact and the water temperature is completely steady. I recommend always cooking foods at a little higher than the minimum temperature and a little longer than the minimum cooking time in order to account for any variance in temperature your equipment causes.

For more information about how long chicken, poultry, and beef need to be held at certain temperatures please refer to the USDA Guide mentioned in our *Resources* chapter. For more explanations of how this works you can reference the excellent guides by Douglas Baldwin[3] or Serious Eats[4] mentioned in our *Resources* chapter.

Plastic Safety

Another main concern of sous vide is cooking in plastic and whether or not this is a dangerous practice. Many scientists and chefs believe that cooking in food grade plastic at these low temperatures does not pose any risk, the temperature is about equivalent to leaving a bottle of water in your car, or in a semi during transport, in summer.

However, I find it hard to believe that we know everything about how plastic reacts to heat, water, our bodies, and the environment. As such, I encourage you to read up on the safety of plastic in sous vide and plastic in general and come to your own conclusions about the safety of using these techniques or consuming products packaged or shipped in plastic.

Sous Vide Equipment

Sous vide cooking doesn't require much equipment, but what you do need can vary greatly in cost and function. Here are the main types of equipment needed and their costs.

We also have up to date information about sous vide equipment available on our website, including reviews.

You can see them here:
www.cookingsousvide.com/info/sous-vide-equipment

Equipment Options

There are two types of equipment you need for sous vide cooking: heat regulators and sous vide pouches. Many people interested in learning sous vide cooking are turned off by the idea of expensive sous vide equipment. While it is true that much of the higher end equipment can get costly, there are now several less-expensive or even free options available.

We look at the entire range of options available when purchasing sous vide equipment, from using a pot on the stove with ziploc bags, to $150 "sous vide controllers", to $1,000 thermal immersion circulators and chambered vacuum sealers.

Just remember, you do not have to bankrupt yourself on expensive sous vide equipment. Start small and test the waters. If you like sous vide cooking then it might be worth spending a little more for some dedicated sous vide equipment.

If you are not concerned with the details of the specific equipment types, feel free to skip ahead to our *Beginning Home Setup* in the next chapter for our complete setup recommendations.

Food Sealers and Sous Vide Pouches

Note: please see the *Plastic Safety* section in our *Sous Vide Safety* chapter for information about cooking in plastic.

Sealing your food in a sous vide pouch accomplishes many things. It can change the texture and density of certain foods. It can also make marinades and seasonings absorb more quickly into the food. However, with most dishes its main purpose is to ensure that the water in the water bath is as close to the food as possible and air is not interfering with the cooking process.

There are many ways to seal your food and here are the most popular methods with their advantages and disadvantages, as well as their corresponding prices. While there are certain applications that can only be accomplished with a powerful vacuum sealer, such as compressing foods, the majority of the sous vide benefits are gained through the low-temperature cooking and not from the sealing itself. This means that for most dishes a food-grade ziploc bag will be just as effective as a chambered vacuum sealer.

Food Grade Ziploc Bags

A great low-cost method of sealing your food is food-grade ziploc bags. They have a few drawbacks but work great for short cooked foods, especially if you are just getting started with sous vide cooking and do not want to spend any up-front money. In most cases sealing your foods with ziploc bags is also a lot easier than using a vacuum sealer.

The ziploc bags will normally have more air in them than the vacuum sealed bags but you can get out almost all of the air by holding the bag underwater, except for the final corner before sealing it. It is also easy to seal in liquids or marinades.

Ziploc bags do run into trouble when used for higher temperature cooking and you will need to check what the bag is rated for before cooking above 150°F to 160°F.

In general I recommend using Ziploc brand bags since they are normally of higher quality than the cheaper brands and hold up better under heat. The freezer Ziplocs with the normal double seal work best in my experience and are normally rated for reheating in the microwave, which is normally at higher temperatures than sous vide.[5]

Food-Grade Plastic Wrap

The other easy method of sealing food for sous vide cooking is to wrap the object in many layers of food grade plastic wrap. This method will allow easy transfer of heat, similar to the vacuum sealed food, but the seal isn't nearly as strong. It will work fine for sous vide cooking for short amounts of time.

This method can also be used to shape foods such as salmon rolls, galantines, and other traditionally cylindrical foods.

Standard Home Vacuum Sealers

Many home cooks prefer a standard home vacuum sealer like a FoodSaver. These vacuum sealers work by inserting the opening of the sous vide food pouch into a small depression in the machine. The sealer then sucks the air out of the pouch and seals it using a heating element. They are the most cost effective method of vacuum sealing your food.

Preparing food with a standard home vacuum sealer gives you the advantage of sucking all the air out of the bag and ensuring maximum heat transfer between the water and the food. The biggest downside to these vacuum sealers is that the process of sucking out the air will also suck out any liquid in the pouch, making it much more difficult to tightly seal foods with marinades. Many home chefs will still use these sealers but seal the bag more loosely if there are marinades or liquids in the pouch, or the liquid can be frozen first.

There are many types of standard vacuum sealers, with Tilia FoodSavers being the most common brand. Tilia FoodSavers make a number of different vacuum sealers, most sold between $100 and $200. Some other less-expensive vacuum sealers are the Rival Seal A Meal and the Deni Vacuum Sealer, though they are usually of lower quality than the FoodSavers[6].

Chambered Vacuum Sealers

The preferred method of sealing your food for professional chefs is to use a chambered vacuum sealer. These industrial vacuum sealers make use of a large vacuum chamber in which the sous vide food pouch is placed. You then close the chamber and all air is removed and the bag is sealed. These are the kind of vacuum sealers normally used in professional kitchens.

The biggest benefit of chambered vacuum sealers is the ability to easily vacuum seal food with liquids or marinades in it, something the lesser sealers have trouble with. Another benefit stems from its finer tuned pressure controls, allowing you to manipulate the density of certain foods. However, these abilities come at a high cost and many chambered vacuum sealers are over $1,500.

Both Industria, PolyScience and MSA sell respected chambered vacuum sealers under their brands and the Minipack-torre MVS31 chamber vacuum sealer is highly regarded.

Temperature Regulation

Proper temperature control of the water bath is critical to effective sous vide cooking. Temperature fluctuations of a few degrees can drastically change the texture of many dishes, especially eggs and fish.

There are several ways to regulate water temperature and we'll discuss the positives and negatives of the main ones. The techniques range from inexpensive and inexact to incredibly precise with the price tag to match.

Thermal Immersion Circulators

A thermal immersion circulator is a heating device that you put into a container of water that will keep the water at a uniform temperature. Thermal circulators were originally developed for use in laboratory work where precision heating is needed for many tasks.

Thermal immersion circulators are probably the best piece of equipment you can get for regulating water temperature in sous vide cooking, but also the most expensive.

How They Work

A standard thermal immersion circulator consists of a heating coil with an attached pump. The heating coil and pump are inserted into a body of water and a temperature is set on the immersion circulator. The heating coil will keep the water at the set temperature while the pump circulates the water to eliminate any hot or cold spots.

Each thermal immersion circulator has its own margin of error for holding the temperature. Most low-end circulators will hold the water at a +/- 1 degree Celsius, while some high-end circulators can hold the temperature to within +/- 0.01 degrees.

Advantages

The biggest benefit of thermal immersion circulators is their precision. Whether the circulator can regulate the heat from within 1 degree celsius or 0.01 degree, it is more than acceptable for perfect sous vide cooking.

Most thermal immersion circulators can also be attached to the edge of a normal kitchen pot, making them very convenient to use in sous vide cooking at home. They can also heat large amounts of water, up to 5x that of some other devices. They also tend to heat very quickly compared to other options.

Disadvantages

The biggest issue with thermal immersion circulators is the high cost of purchasing them. They routinely sell new ones for $800 to $1,500, and used ones are $200 to $600 which is pretty expensive for a piece of home kitchen equipment, especially one specific for sous vide cooking.

A minor negative of thermal immersion circulators is the evaporation due to not having a sealed lid. You can use foil or saran wrap to try and seal it better but you will still suffer some evaporation. This normally isn't a big deal unless you are using a 24+ hour sous vide preparation and then you will have to remember to occasionally add water.

Where to Buy

Probably the best known brand of thermal immersion circulators is PolyScience, who has been tops in the professional market for awhile and has just released an immersion circulator for home chefs sold through Williams-Sonoma[7]. Another well known company is Brinkmann, who makes the Lauda immersion circulators. Sur La Table also has their own line of immersion circulators manufactured by Julabo, both of which normally have high quality equipment.

Another option if you're mechanically inclined is to make one yourself. It can even cost under $100. Seattle Food Geek has put together a great guide for this[8].

You can also look for used thermal immersion circulators on eBay and from scientific lab resell sites. If you do buy a used thermal immersion circulator, be sure to clean it properly since you never know what chemicals were used in it previously.

For that reason, some people refuse to cook with previously used immersion circulators; do so at your own risk.

Thermal Circulating Water Bath

The other heavy duty way to regulate water temperature in sous vide cooking is through the use of a thermal circulating water bath. These devices are similar to the thermal immersion circulators except they come in their own enclosed container for holding the water. Like the immersion circulators, water baths were originally developed for the scientific lab where maintaining precision temperatures can be critical.

How It Works

A normal water bath consists of a lidded container of water with a built in thermal immersion circulator or other heating and circulating device. The container holds the water, and in sous vide cooking the food in a pouch, while the heating unit regulates the temperature of the water and removes all hot and cold spots.

Advantages

Since the circulating water bath has a sealed container it can help reduce evaporation during very long sous vide preparations. They also more easily keep the temperature of the water constant throughout the sous vide process since it is enclosed, requiring less electricity.

Every circulating water bath has its own margin of error for holding the temperature. Most low-end circulators will hold the water at a +/- 1 degree Celsius, while some high-end water baths can hold the temperature to within +/- 0.01 degrees. Either of which is more than enough precision for sous vide cooking.

Disadvantages
Much like the thermal immersion circulators, the largest issue with circulating water baths is their expense. They are also in the $800 to $2,000 range for new equipment.

Where to Buy
PolyScience makes well known thermal water baths[9]. Sur La Table also has a line of circulating water baths.

Another option is the Sous Vide Supreme "water oven" which is basically a non-circulating water bath and has many of the same advantages and disadvantages but it runs at around $400[10].

You can also look for used thermal water baths on eBay and sites that resell scientific lab equipment. If you do buy a used thermal water bath, be sure to clean it well since you never know what chemicals were used in it previously. For that reason, some people refuse to cook with previously used water baths; do so at your own risk.

Sous Vide Cooking Controller
While thermal immersion circulators and thermal circulating water baths are the undisputed leaders of precision temperature control they are out of the price range of many home cooks. Cooking controllers address this issue by providing decent temperature control for a fraction of the price. This device is pretty simple in principal and is used with a rice cooker, crock pot, slow cooker, or other similar device many home cooks have on hand.

How It Works
The sous vide cooking controller is basically a plug with an automated on / off switch that is controlled by a thermometer. Here are the four steps to using it:

1) Take your slow cooker, crock pot or rice cooker and fill it with warm water.

2) Plug your slow cooker into the outlet on the sous vide cooking controller and turn it on to its highest setting.

3) Put the thermometer attached to the cooking controller into the water in the slow cooker.

4) Set the cooking controller temperature display to the temperature you want to maintain during the cooking process.

5) Finally, put the vacuum sealed food into the crock pot and let it cook for the specified time.

The sous vide cooking controller then turns the crock pot on and off to keep the temperature of the water in the slow cooker at a stable temperature.

Advantages

The low price tag is probably the biggest benefit to using a sous vide controller. Most are between $110 and $180, depending on the control desired. Both Auber Instruments and SousVideMagic[11] sell similar types of sous vide controllers that are easily within the price range of most home cooks.

Sous vide controllers are used with your existing crock pots, slow cookers, and rice cookers, check the sous vide controller for specific brands supported. This is definitely a nice convenience and helps save money.

Most sous vide controllers can regulate the temperature to within 1 degree celsius, which is adequate for most sous vide preparations.

Disadvantages

The biggest downside of sous vide controllers is the lack of precision. While most of the producers claim their controllers maintain steady, even heat, they aren't as precise as the more expensive thermal immersion circulators or the thermal water baths, especially in short time frames. This is very noticeable in food like fish and eggs.

However, most people, including us, feel that the sous vide controllers do have enough precision for the home cook to produce excellent results in sous vide cooking, especially for someone looking to try sous vide out before investing large amounts of money.

Where to Buy

SousVideMagic makes a very popular sous vide controller and has very good customer service, tell Frank that CookingSousVide.com sent you. Auber Instruments also sells sous vide controllers for comparable prices. You can also find plans online to make your own.

Sous Vide on the Stove

The cheapest, and least precise, way to do sous vide cooking is directly on your stove. It only requires a stove, a thermometer, some hot water, some cold water, and a good amount of patience.

How It Works

Fill a pot with luke warm water. A larger pot is better since it will hold its temperature when the vacuum sealed sous vide packet is added and it will also be more stable while cooking.

Place a thermometer in the water, preferably a digital meat thermometer with a long cord so the thermometer is convenient and easy to read.

Add either hot water or cold water to bring the pot to the desired temperature. You can also briefly turn a burner on or add ice cubes if you need to move the temperature quickly.

Add the vacuum sealed sous vide packets and bring the water back up to the temperature you need.

Leave the food in the water for as long as the recipe says. Be sure to regularly check the water temperature to make sure it is where you want.

Advantages
The only real advantage of doing sous vide on your stove is that it is very cheap and doesn't require any special equipment.

Disadvantages
Cooking sous vide this way is very imprecise. No matter how diligent you are about checking the water temperature and adjusting it, it will definitely fluctuate by several degrees, and most likely 5-10 degrees. This can play havoc with the texture and doneness of certain types of sous vide food.

It also takes a lot of work to maintain a specific water temperature. You have to constantly be by the water, checking the temperature and adjusting it. This is fine for short cooking sous vide items like fish or some vegetables but for a longer term item it quickly becomes impractical.

Tips for Sous Vide on the Stove
Use a wooden spoon to regularly stir the water, making sure to go up and down as well as side to side. This will help to better even out the temperature of the water.

A larger pot will also hold its temperature better and have a more stable temperature.

"Beer Cooler" Sous Vide
Another very inexpensive way to do sous vide cooking at home is by using the "Beer Cooler" sous vide method. It was first popularized by J. Kenji Lopez-Alt of Series Eats[12]. I'll summarize the method below but for a detailed discussion of it you can view their article directly.

While there are many limitations to "Beer Cooler" sous vide, it is a great way for someone interested in sous vide to try it out without any upfront investment.

How It Works
In general, the beer cooler method takes advantage of a cooler's ability to maintain temperature. You heat water to the temperature you want to cook at and fill the beer cooler with it. At that point you can place the food you are cooking into it, in a sous vide pouch, and close the cooler. Most coolers will maintain its temperature for several hours, cooking the food.

Advantages
The main advantage is price. If you already have a cooler and ziploc bags then it is basically free to try.

Another advantage is that the water coming out of many home faucets is around 131°F-139°F, meaning it is the perfect temperature to cook steak in. If your faucet is in that range it just means you crank up the tap water, fill the cooler, and throw in the steak. It can be very simple.

Disadvantages
If your faucets run cold or you want to cook something at a higher temperature it can be a pain to get the water to the temperature you want.

The temperature also drops, albeit slowly, over time making it unsafe to cook with at the boundaries of food safety. This also makes it hard to cook long-time items with as the temperature will not hold up for multiple days.

Common Sous Vide Setups

With all the options for sous vide equipment available it can be hard to determine how to get stared. Some setups run thousands of dollars while others are only a few hundred. Here are a few of our recommended sous vide setups and the associated costs with each.

Advanced Home Sous Vide Setup

This home sous vide setup has everything you need to create great sous vide results in your own kitchen. It's the most precise method and allows you to have great results on the more finicky dishes like eggs and fish. It also allows you to cook larger amounts of food because of its increased capacity.

If you are looking for a very good home sous vide setup then this one is for you.

Food Sealing

Home vacuum sealers can be found for $125+ and they make sous vide cooking much easier. While they fall short of the power and features of a chambered vacuum sealer they are about a thousand dollars less expensive and bring enough features to make it worth while. There are also many more reasons to get a vacuum sealer. We recommend the FoodSaver V2440, it's not the most recent version but it is consistently the highest rated and is less-expensive than the newer versions[13].

Water Bath and Temperature Control

For this home sous vide setup we recommend an immersion circulator. They are very, very precise, heat up fast, and can heat large amounts of water. We have used the PolyScience Sous Vide Professional, which is built for the home cooks, but there are other circulators with high marks as well[14].

For your water bath you can either use a large pot or we suggest getting a sous vide

water tub. They look like plastic storage tubs but are food grade quality. They normally run from $20 to $40 and will allow you to cook a larger amount of food than in a pot.

Cooking the Food

With this sous vide setup there are only two "hands-on" cooking moments required. The first is to preheat the water bath, this will help to keep a steady temperature in the water bath due to the way the sous vide controller works. The second is during long-cooking dishes when you occasionally rotate the food in the water bath, about every 6-10 hours if possible, and add some fresh water. That is all the effort you have to expend to have very high-quality sous vide food.

Total Cost

- Vacuum Sealer: $150
- Immersion Circulator: $800-$1000
- Water Tab: $20 - $40
Total Cost: $1000 - $1,200 for the complete setup

Beginning Home Sous Vide Setup

This home sous vide setup has everything you need to create decent sous vide results in your own kitchen. It's by far the most cost efficient method for the home cook and requires very little effort to set up and use.

While this method can cost several hundred dollars to set up from scratch, many cooks already have some of the equipment on hand. Most of the equipment in this setup can also be reused for non-sous vide purposes so they are not just a single-technique item.

If you are looking for an inexpensive but relatively effective sous vide setup then this one is for you.

Food Sealing

For beginning sous vide it makes sense to start off with ziploc bags, as long as you feel comfortable using them. If you feel the need to upgrade to a vacuum sealer then you can approach that at a later date.

Water Bath and Temperature Control #1

If you already have a large crock pot or rice cooker then we recommend using this Water Bath and Temperature Control.

The best water bath is a typical self-heating device, rice cookers are the best but crock pots also work very well. As long as the chamber is big enough for the size of food you will normally be cooking then you should be fine. If you currently own a rice cooker or crock pot then go ahead and use it, if not then I recommend starting with a rice cooker because it has better distribution of heat.

The most cost-effective way to control temperature is with a sous vide controller. There are many different brands but SousVideMagic has a good reputation and focuses almost exclusively on sous vide cooking. The sous vide controller works by measuring the temperature of your water bath and turning your heating device (the crock pot or rice cooker) on and off to maintain a consistent temperature. I've had great results with this even for short ribs that were cooked for over 48 hours.

Water Bath and Temperature Control #2

If you do not have a large crock pot or rice cooker then we recommend looking into the Sous Vide Supreme[15]. It is about the same cost as buying a SousVideMagic and a good rice cooker. It looks a little more professional or "appliance like" sitting on your counter and has very good temperature controls. Either this or the SousVideMagic will work well for you to get started.

Cooking the Food

With this sous vide setup there are only two "hands-on" cooking moments required. The first is to preheat the water bath, this will help to keep a steady temperature in the water bath due to the way the sous vide controller works. The second is during long-cooking dishes when you occasionally rotate the food in the water bath, about every 6-10 hours if possible. That is all the effort you have to expend to have very high-quality sous vide food.

Total Cost
- Ziploc Bags: $5
- Sous Vide Controller: $150
- Crock Pot / Rice Cooker: $150
- or Sous Vide Supreme: $450
Total Cost: $300 to $450 for a complete sous vide set up, assuming you don't have any of the equipment already.

Cheap Sous Vide Setup

One of the big misconceptions about sous vide cooking is that you have to spend thousands of dollars to do it. While it is possible to spend that much money you can also get a very good sous vide setup for much cheaper, or even for free.

This cheap sous vide setup can be applied to many dishes that don't require long amounts of cooking time such as many vegetables or most types of fish. However, you can't use this setup for most types of meat because of the constant work required to maintain the proper temperature and the fluctuations in temperature.

Food Sealing
For the cheap sous vide setup you can wrap the food in food-grade plastic wrap several layers thick, or even use a food-grade ziploc bag with all the air removed. If you already have a vacuum sealer such as a FoodSaver around then definitely use it to seal the food.

Water Bath
The cheapest way to set up a water bath is to use a pot of water on your stove. A large pot is easier to work with than a small pot since

it maintains its temperature better. You can also try out the "Sous Vide Beer Cooler" trick[16].

Temperature Control

Working with a thermometer it is pretty easy to maintain a temperature within a few degrees to either side of your ideal temperature. Leaving the stove on low, or turning it on and off, and adding ice cubes or cold water in small amounts allows you to keep the water temperature relatively stable. It won't stay within the .1 degree range that many devices can maintain but for short amounts of time it will do just fine.

I recommend using a meat thermometer with a cord, that way it's easy to keep it out of the way while you regulate the water temperature.

Cooking the Food

Once you put the food in the water, try to maintain the temperature that you are aiming for as closely as possible and you'll need to cook most dishes for 15 to 20 minutes, or up to an hour. Anything longer begins to become unmanageable.

Total Cost

About $25 for a thermometer if you don't already have one, otherwise it is basically a free method to try sous vide cooking.

This method of cheap sous vide is more time and effort intensive than other methods. However, it's a great place to experiment and see if you want to invest the few hundred dollars to move up to a basic "hands-off" set up with a sous vide controller that we recommend in the *Beginning Home Sous Vide Setup* section.

Tips and Tricks

While the majority of sous vide cooking is relatively simple, there are still many things to keep in mind that can increase your chances of success. Many of these tips also relate to all cooking methods.

For more tips and tricks you can visit our sous vide forums.
There's a lot of questions answered and information exchanged there.

You can find them on our website here:
www.cookingsousvide.com/sous-vide-forums

Flavor

Always Salt and pepper

Salt and peppering your food before vacuum sealing it will only enhance the flavors of the finished meal. It's recommended for almost every dish to add salt and pepper before cooking it and as you are finishing it. Don't be afraid to taste your dishes as they come together to make sure they are properly seasoned.

Use Good Salt

Not all salts are made equal. For most recipes you should use kosher salt unless specified otherwise. Kosher salt isn't very expensive and the difference in taste and texture is very apparent. Also, stay away from the iodized salt, it will often impart a chemical flavor to your foods that can be off-putting.

Easy on the Spices

Because of the length of time sous vide cooking requires, especially for the tough cuts of meat, and the effects of the vacuum seal, spices can come across much stronger than they would in a roast or braise. It's better to err of the side of less and re-season after taking them out of the sous vide bath than to try and eat a dish that tastes like raw garlic.

Ingredients, Ingredients, Ingredients

You want to know what the secret to good cooking is? Use high-quality ingredients. The better the ingredients you use the better your resulting dish will be. This is even easier with sous vide since you will be perfectly cooking the food every time and don't have to worry about ruining it.

More and more farmers markets are opening up in cities everywhere[17] and if you are planning a nice meal the extra flavor from locally grown fruits and vegetables (and even meat) is more than worth the extra money.

Fresh is Better

Another way to improve your dishes is to be sure to use fresh ingredients. If a recipe calls for lime or orange juice, instead of using bottled juice just grab a lime and juice it for the recipe, you'll be able to taste the difference.

Turn to the Powders

Using fresh herbs and spices instead of dried is normally a good idea when cooking. However, with sous vide it can be better to use the dried powders in some cases. This is especially true for things like garlic and ginger because the raw form of both can sometimes create a bitterness in the final dish.

Give it Some Smoke

If you are preparing a BBQ-style dish it can help if you smoke the meat before sealing it. Even 30-60 minutes in the smoker can add a lot of flavor to the final dish. It's normally better to smoke the food before cooking it as opposed to afterwards.

Cheat on the Smoke

If you don't have a smoker or the time to smoke your food there is a quicker way to add some smokiness. Instead of smoking it you can add a small amount of Liquid Smoke to the bag prior to it being sealed. A smoking gun[18] can also be a very useful tool.

Don't Forget the Brine

Even though sous vide cooking traps most of the moisture and flavor in the food it never hurts to brine your chicken or pork first as it will result in even more tender and flavorful meat. For an easy brine mix 1 cup of salt, ½ cup of sugar, and 1 gallon of water, bring to a boil for 5 minutes, cool completely, then fully submerge the meat in it for 4-12 hours depending on the size of the meat. You can also add spices or herbs for additional flavor, like rosemary, thyme, peppercorns, or bay leaves which will transfer through the brine into the meat.

Hold the Booze

Alcohol based marinades are a classic way to cook, from bourbon in BBQ sauce to red wine in braises. However, when it comes to sous vide you can run into trouble with a marinade that has alcohol in it. Because of the low temperature and the sealed bag the alcohol will not evaporate off which can lead to a dish that has a harsh alcohol flavor instead of the mellow undertones.

Tailor to Your Guests

Since sous vide dishes can be cooked in individual pouches it allows you to tailor the portions to who is eating them. For instance, if someone is allergic to pepper or spices you can do one pouch without the pepper and the other pouches with it.

You can also use two or three different seasonings in a batch of sous vide by sealing them separately. Then you can let everyone mix and match and eat the ones they prefer.

Remove the Fat

Since sous vide cooking does not get up to high temperatures (about 145°F to 150°F) it does not render fat nearly as well as other cooking techniques. When it comes to dishes cooked over a long period of time, such as short ribs or a roast, be sure to remove any extra fat from the meat before cooking it. This will result in a much leaner and more tender meat with a lot better texture.

Sealing

Don't Stuff The Pouches

In order to ensure proper cooking it's important to make sure the thickness of the food in your pouches is relatively even. Don't force in extra food or layer the food in the pouches. It's better to use multiple pouches with a single layer of food than one large pouch. Most recipes assume a single layer of food when determining the cooking time.

Airtight Ziplocs

If you are using ziploc bags to seal your food you can use this trick to force out the majority of the air. Once the bag is ready to close, seal the bag except for 1" of it. Place the bag into the water bath making sure to keep that last 1" out of the water. The water will force the remaining air out of the bag and then you can seal it completely. When done properly this is almost as good as using a weak vacuum sealer and will work great for most low-temperature sous vide cooking.

Freeze the Liquids

If you need to seal liquids in a bag and you can't seal the bag because of it one easy method is to freeze the liquids first. Then you can add them to the sous vide pouch and seal it. Once the food is in the water bath the liquid will unfreeze and work its magic. Two things to remember: 1) alcohol won't freeze and 2) if there is a large amount of liquid the seal on the bag won't be very tight because liquids are more dense than ice.

Low Temperature + Liquid = Ziplocs

If you need to seal liquid into a sous vide pouch and you are cooking it in a low temperature bath the easiest thing to do is to use ziploc bags as the pouch. Using the Airtight ziplocs tip you can get as good as a vacuum as you will be able to with a conventional vacuum sealer and avoid any potential mess.

Need Liquids? Use the Override

Many vacuum sealers have an override switch to seal the bag at it's current vacuum state. If you need to seal liquids in the sous vide pouch and you are using a high-temperature dish or you don't want to use ziplocs then you can use this to remove a lot of air from the sous vide pouches.

Fill the sous vide pouch with the food and liquid. Place it in your vacuum sealer and then hang it off of a counter, so the liquid is as far away from the sealer as possible. Be sure to support the bottom of the bag so you don't have a mess on your hands. Then begin the vacuuming process, watching the level of the liquid. As soon as the liquid nears the top of the sous vide pouch hit the "Seal" button, which should seal the pouch without pulling the liquid all the way out.

Cooking

Preheat the Water

Preheating your water is very important for dishes that are cooked for a short amount of time. The temperature of the water can fluctuate wildly during the first 30-60 minutes, especially with cheaper sous vide setups, and can adversely affect the outcome of your dish if it is only in the water that long. For sous vide dishes that are cooked for five hours or more it isn't as important but preheating never hurts.

Heavy on the Water

This is an important tip, especially for items cooked over a short period of time. Even if you preheat the water, when you put the colder food into the water bath the temperature will drop and the heating element will go into overdrive to bring it back up to temperature. The more water you are cooking in the less the temperature will drop. It can also help to let your food sit out for 15-30 minutes to come up to a higher temperature so the change in the water won't be as severe.

Turn Up the Heat

Most meat cooked sous vide should be done with very un-fatty cuts. However, if you find yourself with a more fatty cut you can turn the temperature up to about 150°F which will help break down the collagen without drying it out completely. The same cut of meat cooked at 130°F will actually be tougher because of the excess of collagen.

All Meat is Different

More and more people are purchasing meat from places other than the supermarket for a variety of reasons from better flavor and texture to healthier meat and more humane treatment. I'll save any lectures for another time but one thing is apparent, meat raised in different ways behaves differently when cooked. We've found that grass-fed beef roasts only need to be cooked for about one half the time of a comparable supermarket roast before they become tender. So be aware that meat from different places cooks differently, there's nothing worse than turning an expensive cut of meat to mush.

Separate the Skin

If you love crispy skin, whether it's for chicken, duck, or fish, it can be hard to crisp properly with sous vide. A great work around is to remove the skin before you cook the food. Then as it gets close to time to remove the food from the water bath you can put the skin in the oven on a raised sheet pan and cook it at 350°F to 400°F for 15 to 20 minutes for super-crispy skin. Just place it on top of the food when you serve it and no one will ever know you cheated.

Finishing

Drier the Better

When searing, you want your meat to be as dry as possible to speed up the searing process. The easiest way to accomplish this is to use paper towels or a dish towel to pat the meat dry. This works when cooking raw meat that has been in a marinade as well. I have specially colored dish towels that I only use for this purpose and wash after each time.

Crank the Heat

When searing foods that have already been cooking sous vide you want to minimize the amount of time they are on the grill or in the pan. If using a grill turn it as hot as it can go and only cook the meat until a crust develops, no more than 1 or 2 minutes per side.

If you are using a hot pan, heat it until the oil just begins to smoke and then place the meat in. Once again, just leave it in until the meat begins to sear, no more than 1 or 2 minutes a side.

Preheat the Searer

Whether you are finishing your sous vide meat on a grill, on a stove, or in the oven under the broiler you should always preheat it. Putting the meat in a cold pan or grill just takes it longer to sear and cooks the meat a lot more. Using only preheated things helps keep the cooking to the outside of the meat, leaving the inside perfectly cooked.

Bring Out the Blow Torch

If you have a pastry blow torch you can use it to sear the finished meat instead of pan-frying or grilling. Be warned though, it can be hard to sear chicken with a torch without burning it.

Open the Grill Lid

Often times when cooking on the grill, especially for thicker foods, you'll close the lid to keep the heat in and more evenly cook the food. When you're searing your sous vided foods you should leave the lid open, minimizing the cooking that will happen except on the side being seared.

Simple Salsas are Great

If you are cooking a normal weekday meal then a quick and easy way to finish off sous vided meat is to just add a simple salsa to the top of it. This is especially easy in summer. Simply chop up some fresh vegetables like tomatoes, corn, avocado or squash and some herbs like basil or oregano and toss together with some olive oil and a splash of apple cider or red wine vinegar. Plate the salsa on the meat and you are all done, and the dish even looks fancy.

Time Saving

Save it for Later

Most sous vide meals can be first cooked and then quickly chilled to be reheated later. To chill most food take them directly out of the sous vide bath and place the pouch in a ice-water bath until cold.

Make and Freeze Your Own Steaks

Because of the ability of sous vide to transform tough cuts of meat into very tender "steaks" some people will cook a chuck roast with sous vide, cool it, then slice it into 1" thick slices and freeze them. When they're ready to eat they remove a slice from the freezer, defrost it, and sear on the grill or in a pan. It can be a good way to transform a cheap cut of meat into the equivalent of a much more expensive steak.

Fast Preheating

A simple way to preheat the water in your sous vide bath is to fill it ½ way full with room temperature water, then heat 3-4 cups of water in the microwave. Then you can fill the water bath the rest of the way with a mixture of the hot water and the room temperature water, watching the thermometer to make sure the temperature stays near where you need it to be.

Freezer Steaks

A lot of time sous vide cooking is thought of as upscale food when in reality it can be hugely convenient. One simple method is to buy steaks (or chicken or pork) in bulk then season, vacuum seal and freeze them. When you need a simple meal just take one or two of the steaks out of the freezer and put them directly in the water bath for a few hours. Throw together a quick salad and you have a great meal all ready.

Take Advantage of the Time Frames

A great thing about sous vide is that it's harder to over cook your food. Take advantage of this fact when you don't know when you'll be eating. Often on weekends my wife and I do yard work and we know we want to eat afterwards but have no idea when we will finish. Throwing some steaks in the sous vide bath before we get started allows us to have great food waiting for us when we're done, whether it is in 3 hours or 6 hours. Plus, it saves on a lot of cooking time when we're beat from working all day!

A Word About Our Recipes

For each section of sous vide dish types we've included several recipes to help get you started. For all of our recipes we used either ziploc bags or a FoodSaver vacuum sealer and a SousVideMagic or PolyScience Sous Vide Professional. This means that regardless of your sous vide setup, all of the recipes in this book should be doable.

How to Use the Recipes

Read the Recipe FIRST

This might sound like a no-brainer but with sous vide it is very important to read the whole recipe before starting. Many recipes require marinades or other initial steps and often times you need to start working on the finishing portion of the recipe while the meat is still cooking. Just read through the recipe first, make sure you understand it, and then you won't run into any surprises down the road.

Sous Vide Pouches

In the recipes we just say "Add the food to the sous vide pouches". This can be any type of sous vide pouch you feel comfortable using, from plastic wrap or ziplocs up to industrial food pouches.

It also assumes that you are using as many sous vide pouches as you need for the food to lay in one even layer, usually less than 2" thick. If spices or liquids are added to the pouches then just split them evenly between all the pouches.

Salt And Pepper

Most of the recipes call for "Salt and pepper" as an ingredient. Proper seasoning is critical to good cooking and you should salt and pepper your ingredients before they go into the pouches, when they come out, and as you are making any finishing steps.

While we'd like to give you specific measurements, how much you use is in large part a matter of taste. And since studies show this likely differs across people through genetics and upbringing, we

haven't given specifics. Be sure to taste your food as you go and you should be fine.

Time and Temperatures

Our recipes just give you a single temperature and a time range for each dish. The temperatures are based on our personal preferences and are usually on the medium-rare side. If you prefer food cooked more or less you can refer to our comprehensive *Time and Temperature Charts* for the cut of meat used in that dish.

You can also apply recipes to other cuts of meat in the same way, like taking a steak recipe and using it for chicken. Just find the cut of meat you'd like to use in the *Time and Temperature Charts* and use the values given instead of the ones in the recipe.

Quantities

There are many different types of recipes in this book. Some are for sides, some are main courses and some are for complete meals. The "Serves" number we give you tries to take into account what the dish is used for. A recipe for mashed potatoes might serve 4 but we are assuming you will serve it as a side with other things and not just by itself on a plate. Read through the recipe first and you should be fine.

Experimenting

We hope you will use these recipes to get acquainted with the sous vide process and use them as a launching pad for developing your own recipes. Part of the fun of cooking is creating your own dishes and our recipes are meant to be inspirational, not followed to the letter.

Temperature

As long as you read and understand the safety section for each type of meat and stay above the lower temperature threshold you can vary the temperature you use to cook your dishes. Some people love a 135°F chicken breast and others, me included, prefer it around 141°F to 145°F. Try different temperatures and see what you like best.

Time

As long as you leave it in for the minimum amount of time needed for safety, time is probably the least important part of sous vide cooking. In general, the longer something is cooked the more tender it will be but a steak is usually good anywhere from 1 to 6 hours after being in the bath.

Roasts can be cooked well in a 20 to 30 hour window. Experiment with the times that dishes are cooked for and see what works for you. And if something needs to come out sooner, after it reaches the safety time, then go ahead, it might not be quite as tender but it should still be great.

Ingredients

Ingredients are largely a matter of taste and are the easiest things to experiment with. If a recipe calls for an ingredient you don't like or don't have, feel free to omit it or add your own. Add more or less of a spice to your preferences. Prefer parsley to basil? Then go ahead and substitute.

If you use great ingredients and cook them well it's hard to go wrong.

Beef Roasts and Tough Cuts

When it comes to beef, the roasts and other tough cuts can show dramatic results in cooking. We cover the majority of cuts that you will find at your butcher

Overview

Some of the most impressive results of sous vide are created with tough cuts of beef. Sous vide allows you to do things that traditional methods are unable to accomplish, such as cooking short ribs medium-rare but still tenderizing them, or creating fall-apart medium-rare roasts.

This is accomplished because cooking tough cuts of beef with sous vide allows you to break down and tenderize the meat without cooking it above medium-rare and drying it out. Once temperatures in beef go above 140°F the meat begins to dry out and become more bland. However, they also start to tenderize more quickly above this temperature which is why tough roasts and braises are done for hours at high temperatures. Using sous vide, you can hold the meat below 140°F for a long enough time for the tenderizing process to run its course.

I often use sous vide cooked beef as a basis for many normal beef dishes, such as pot roast, beef stew, goulash, chili, or corned beef. You can also use it in any of your favorite recipes, simply replace the cooking step in the recipe with the already cooked sous vide beef and then continue the rest of the recipe.

Time and Temperature Guidelines

The FDA states that beef is safe when it is held at 130°F for over 112 minutes, or 140°F for over 12 minutes. This is very easy to do with sous vide and the main reason we recommend cooking most beef cuts

medium-rare since beef is most tender at that temperature[19].

Additionally, the center of "whole" muscles are sterile but due to some mechanical tenderization that some meat packagers use the muscles can be compromised so unless you trust your supplier it is advisable to cook beef to 130°F throughout.

Medium-rare beef is cooked between 130°F to 139°F, though we recommend cooking it at 131°F to give yourself a few degrees of temperature variation above the bottom of the safe zone. Feel free to experiment with any temperatures in that range. Depending on the toughness of the cut of beef, it may need to be cooked anywhere from 4 hours up to 2 or 3 days.

For each beef cut we also give directions for medium in our *Time and Temperature Charts*, these are normally cooked between 140°F and 149°F, though we recommend not going above 140°F because the beef begins drying out quickly and with sous vide there is no gain in food safety above 131°F.

Also, some beef cuts benefit from higher temperatures to help further tenderize them. These dishes will result in a more traditional look and feel from the cut of meat and we have provided these for several of the cuts. These "Well / Traditional" entries in our *Time and Temperature Charts* will be "fork tender" like a normal braise would be.

Most tough cuts of beef are cooked sous vide for between 1 and 2 days. However, for some more tender beef roasts shorter cooking times of 4 to 8 hours will be enough time to tenderize the meat fully. It is also good to keep in mind that different quality of meat cooks at different speeds, for instance most grass fed beef cooks faster and needs less time to tenderize.

General Process

The normal method of cooking tough cuts of beef with sous vide is very simple. If the meat is over 3" wide slice it into 2" strips, if you want the roast to stay whole it is possible but you will need to add some cooking time to it.

Preheat your water bath to the temperature desired, we recommend 131°F to 140°F for most cuts unless you are trying the "Well / Traditional" entry.

Take the meat and sprinkle it with salt and pepper and seal it into a sous vide pouch. You can also season the meat before sealing it with any normal seasoning such as:

- Fresh or dried thyme or rosemary
- Any spice powders such as onion, garlic, or paprika
- Chile powders like ancho, chipotle, cayenne
- Marinades, though you don't need much
- Sauces like A1 steak, worcester sauce, BBQ sauce, etc.

If adding a sauce or marinade make sure your vacuum sealer does not suck it out, you can normally seal it before all the air is out to prevent this just fine. Also, we do not recommend using fresh garlic, onions, or

ginger, as they can begin to take on a bad flavor over the long cooking times.

After sealing the pouch place it into the water bath for the indicated cooking time.

Once it's fully cooked remove it from the pouch and pat dry. At this point you can sear the meat in a hot skillet to add a nice crust to it or you can slice it and serve as is. You can also apply a normal roast crust such as a garlic paste or horseradish and place it in a very hot oven until the crust sets, about 5 to 10 minutes.

Once the meat is done cooking you can use it as you would any roast or braise. You can also make a nice gravy or pan sauce from the liquid leftover in the sous vide pouch.

Recipe Notes

Most of the cuts of meat used in these recipes are completely interchangeable with each other. Just adjust the cooking time accordingly.

Times are expressed in a wide range depending on the toughness of the roast. The meat will be tasty at the lower end of the range but will get more tender as you near the top of it. Choose the time that fits your schedule and your taste.

Remember that grass-fed beef will often times tenderize much faster than store bought steaks.

Garlic-Rosemary Sirloin Roast

Time: 12 to 24 Hours
Temperature: 131°F / 55°C
Serves: 4-6

For the Sous Vide Roast
3-4 pound sirloin roast
1 tablespoon garlic powder
1 tablespoon paprika powder
¼ tablespoon ancho chile powder
2 thyme sprigs
2 rosemary sprigs

For the Crust
8 garlic cloves, peeled
4 rosemary sprigs
4 thyme sprigs
2-4 tablespoons sweet marjoram
2-4 tablespoons olive oil

*One of my favorite meals is a good roast beef.
However, roasts are notoriously hard to cook properly.
People are split on the best method to create a good
outer crust while still keeping the middle a good
temperature. Even the best roasts have a wide band
around them of overcooked meat. Sous vide comes to
the rescue once again.*

*Cooking with sous vide allows you to keep the entire
roast the doneness you want. For extra flavor you can
apply a rub or paste to the outside of the roast and
quickly sear or broil it to form a nice crust. I prefer a
nice garlic, rosemary, and thyme paste but many
people love a horseradish or mustard crust on their
roast beef.*

*I used a sirloin roast for this sous vide recipe but you
can use any large roast cut of beef. For some of the
tougher cuts of beef you might want to increase the
time spent in the sous vide.*

Pre-Bath
Preheat the water bath to 131°F / 55°C.

Cover the sirloin roast with salt, pepper, the
garlic, paprika and ancho chile powders and
place in a pouch. Add the thyme and
rosemary to the sous vide pouch and then
seal. Place the sirloin roast in the water bath
and cook for 12 to 24 hours.

Finishing
40 to 60 minutes before the roast is done
wrap the garlic cloves in aluminum foil with
some olive oil and salt and place in a 400°F
oven for 30 to 45 minutes, until soft. Remove
and set aside to cool.

Turn the oven to 450°F or 500°F.

Right before the sous vide roast is done
make the paste for the crust. Combine all the
crust ingredients in a food processor and
pulse until it forms a thick paste.

Take the sous vide sirloin roast out of the
water bath and remove it from the pouch.
Pat it dry with a paper towel or dish cloth
and place in a roasting pan. Smear the sides
and top of the meat with the paste. Place the
roast in the oven until the crust is done,
about 5 minutes.

Remove the roast from the oven, cut it into
thin slices and serve. It goes well with
mashed potatoes, a side salad, or mixed
vegetables.

Dry Rubbed BBQ Beef

Time: 1 to 2 Days
Temperature: 131°F / 55°C
Serves: 4 to 6

For the Beef
2-3 pounds top round roast, cut into 1 ½″ slabs
1 cup BBQ sauce

For the Rub
5 tablespoons brown sugar
4 tablespoons salt
¼ cup paprika
3 tablespoons freshly ground black pepper
1 ½ tablespoons onion powder
1 ½ tablespoons garlic powder
½ teaspoon mustard powder
½ teaspoon cayenne pepper
½ teaspoon celery seeds

This sweet rub has a hint of heat and works well on most kinds of beef. It's also good on chicken and pork. Using a tough cut of beef like this for steaks helps save money, especially when cooking for a large number of people. The sous vide process will help tenderize it enough that it will taste like a higher quality steak.

Pre-Bath
Preheat the water bath to 131°F / 55°C.

Mix together all the rub ingredients in a bowl then coat the roast with it. Any extra rub can be kept in a sealed container in a cabinet for several months.

Add the roast slabs to the sous vide pouches and then seal. Place in the water bath for 1 to 2 days. For a grass-fed roast 12 to 24 hours should be good.

Finishing
Preheat a grill to very hot.

Take the beef slabs out of the water bath and remove them from the pouches. Pat them dry with a paper towel or dish cloth. Quickly sear the slabs on the grill for about 1 to 2 minutes per side. Brush both sides with the BBQ sauce and grill for 30 seconds on each side.

Take the beef off the grill, slice into strips and serve. It is great served with macaroni and cheese, coleslaw, or potato salad. It is also excellent when sliced and served on some fresh rolls with cheddar cheese and more BBQ sauce.

Sous Vide Corned Beef and Cabbage

Time: 24 to 48 Hours
Temperature: 135°F / 57°C
Serves: 4

3-4 pounds of corned beef
1 head of cabbage, cut into ½" wide strips
6 slices of bacon, cut into ¼" strips
1-2 cups fresh chicken stock
¼ cup white wine vinegar

Corned beef cooked with sous vide results in meat with a great texture. It is also much juicier and more flavorful than many corned beefs.

In this recipe we call for it to be cooked at 135°F which was the temperature we liked best. However, our test with the corned beef cooked at 146°F was also very good. It was drier than the 135°F meat but a bit more tender. Either temperature will result in fantastic corned beef.

Pre-Bath

Preheat your sous vide water bath to 135°F / 57°C.

Seal the corned beef in a sous vide pouch and place the pouch into your water bath. Let it cook for 24 to 48 hours.

Finishing

About 45 minutes before you are ready to eat begin to prepare the cabbage.

Cook the bacon strips over medium heat until crisp and the fat is rendered. Pour out all but 1-2 tablespoons of the bacon fat.

Add the cabbage strips to the bacon pan and cook over medium-high heat for about 5 minutes. Add 1 cup of the chicken stock and the ¼ cup of vinegar to the pan. Let the cabbage cook in the liquid until tender, adding more chicken stock if it begins to dry out.

When the cabbage starts to become tender, remove the corned beef from the water bath and the sous vide pouch. Slice the corned beef into ½" - ¾" slices.

Serve the corned beef on a plate with the cabbage piled on top of it. This is also wonderful when served with roasted potatoes, fresh bread, or a light salad.

Beef Goulash

Time: 12 to 24 Hours
Temperature: 131°F / 55°C
Serves: 4

2 pounds stew meat or chuck roast cut into 1"
chunks
½ teaspoon garlic powder
1 large onion, diced
2 green peppers, diced
4 garlic cloves, diced
2 tablespoons paprika
1 package baby bella or button mushrooms,
diced
2 14-ounce cans of diced tomatoes
1 cup beef stock
2 tablespoons flour
4 tablespoons cold water
2 tablespoons chopped fresh parsley

*This sous vide beef Goulash is a great wintertime dish
and is really hardy, especially when served with a
good sticky rice or mashed potatoes. The beef is first
cooked sous vide and only added to the goulash itself
near the end, ensuring the meat is not overcooked.*

*We only cook the beef for 24 hours so the resulting
meat isn't meltingly tender. We've found that beef
chunks that are the typical sous vide tenderness do
not have the chewy bite that is ideal in stews and chili
and leaves the end dish lacking. The reduced cooking
time leaves some of the chewiness while still
tenderizing a majority of the meat.*

Pre-Bath
Preheat the water bath to 131°F /55°C.

Season the meat with salt and pepper,
sprinkle with the garlic powder then seal in
the sous vide pouch and place in the water
bath. Cook for 12 to 24 hours.

Finishing
You will start to make the goulash itself
about 30 to 45 minutes before you want to
eat.

Heat up some oil in a deep frying pan or
pot. Add the onion and garlic and saute for
several minutes, until they begin to get
translucent. Add the green peppers and
paprika and saute for another 2 minutes.

Remove the onions and pepper mixture
from the pan and add some more oil and the
mushrooms. After a few minutes the
mushrooms should begin to brown and
release their liquid.

Add the onion and pepper mixture back to
the pan with the mushrooms and add the
tomatoes and beef stock. Stir to mix and let
simmer for 10-15 minutes so the flavors can
meld and the sauce can thicken slightly.

Mix the cold water with the flour and add
gradually to the goulash, mixing thoroughly,
until it becomes the thickness you desire.

Remove the sous vide beef from the water
bath and add to the goulash, along with the
liquids. Add the parsley to the goulash, mix
well, and then serve.

Red Wine Marinated Beef Ribs

Time: 2 to 3 Days
Temperature: 137°F / 58.3°C
Serves: 4 to 8

3 to 4 pounds of beef ribs

For the marinade
2 cups red wine
2 cups water
½ cup salt
½ cup brown sugar
1-2 tablespoons chipotle powder

This marinade helps infuse the ribs with even more moisture and flavor than they normally have. You can also play around with the spices in the marinade and see what flavors you like best. It's simple and fast to put together. These ribs go well with roasted vegetables and polenta.

Pre-Bath

Whisk together all of the marinade ingredients. Put the ribs into one or more ziploc bags and pour the marinade over top. Place in the refrigerator for 3 to 5 hours.

Preheat the water bath to 137°F / 58.3°C.

Remove the ribs from the marinade and place them into the sous vide pouches. Seal the pouches and place in the water bath. Cook for 2 to 3 days.

Finishing

Take the ribs out of the water bath and remove them from the pouches. Pat them dry with a paper towel or dish cloth. Quickly sear the ribs on the grill or pan for about 1 to 2 minutes per side, until just browned. Remove from the heat and serve.

BBQ Beef Brisket

Time: 1 to 3 Days
Temperature: 135°F / 57.2°C
Serves: 4 to 8

3-4 pound brisket
1 tablespoon liquid smoke

For the Rub
2 tablespoons ground cumin
2 tablespoons garlic powder
2 tablespoons onion powder
2 tablespoons ground coriander
1 teaspoon chipotle powder

If you enjoy smoking foods you can omit the liquid smoke and then manually smoke the brisket before you put it in the water bath. This brisket is great with any normal BBQ sides like cole slaw or potato salad. For even more flavor you can serve it with your favorite BBQ sauce. Leftovers are fantastic on nice rolls when topped with melted cheese, diced onions, and BBQ sauce.

Pre-Bath
Preheat the water bath to 135°F / 57.2°C.

Mix together all the rub ingredients in a bowl then coat the brisket with it. Any extra rub can be kept in a sealed container in a cabinet for several months.

Add the brisket to the sous vide pouch along with the liquid smoke and then seal. Place in the water bath for 1 to 3 days. For a grass-fed roast 24 to 36 hours should be good.

Finishing
Preheat a grill to very hot.

Take the brisket out of the water bath and remove it from the pouch. Pat it dry with a paper towel or dish cloth. Quickly sear the brisket on the grill for about 1 to 2 minutes per side.

Take the brisket off the grill, slice into ⅛" to ¼" strips, and serve.

Tuscan Roast Beef

Time: 3 to 6 Hours
Temperature: 131°F / 55°C
Serves: 4 to 8

3 pounds whole tenderloin or tenderloin roast

For the Rub
¼ cup fresh rosemary
¼ cup fresh parsley
3 tablespoons fresh oregano
2 tablespoons fresh sage
2 garlic cloves, coarsely chopped
2 tablespoons salt
2 tablespoons black pepper
½ cup olive oil

This recipe uses bold herbs to add a lot of flavor to the normally blander tenderloin. For another variation you can add the juices from the pouch to a cup or two of chicken or beef stock and reduce it into a gravy.

Pre-Bath
Preheat the water bath to 131°F / 55°C.

First make the Tuscan rub by putting all of the rub ingredients into a food processor and process until mixed.

Rub the roast with the Tuscan rub and place in the sous vide pouch. Seal the pouch and place in the water bath for 3 to 6 hours.

Finishing
Preheat a grill or pan to very hot.

Take the roast out of the water bath and remove it from the pouches. Pat it dry with a paper towel or dish cloth. Quickly sear the slabs on the grill or pan for 1 to 2 minutes per side.

Take the roast off the grill and serve as you would a normal roast. It is great with mashed potatoes, brussels sprouts, or green beans.

Short Ribs with Basil-Balsamic Sauce

Time: 36 to 48 Hours
Temperature: 137°F / 57°C
Serves: 4

For the Ribs
3-4 pounds of short ribs
2 teaspoons garlic powder
2 teaspoons onion powder
4 rosemary sprigs
4 thyme sprigs
Salt and pepper

For the Sauce
3 tablespoons balsamic vinegar
½ teaspoon finely minced garlic
⅓ cup fresh basil leaves
½ cup olive oil
Salt and pepper

2 tablespoons fresh basil leaves, coarsely chopped, for garnish

These short ribs have a nice tang to them from the sauce. Cooking them at the slightly higher temperature allows them to break down even more while still not over cooking. They go well with a side of mashed potatoes or roasted vegetables.

Pre-Bath

Preheat your sous vide water bath to 137°F / 57°C.

Salt and pepper the ribs and sprinkle with the garlic and onion powders. Place in a sous vide pouch and add the thyme and rosemary. Seal the pouches and place in your water bath. Let it cook for 36 to 48 hours.

Finishing

Place all the ingredients for the sauce into a blender or food processor and process until thoroughly combined.

Remove the short ribs from the sous vide pouches and pat them dry with a paper towel or dish cloth. Quickly sear the ribs on hot grill or in a hot pan for about 1 to 2 minutes per side, until just browned.

Place the ribs on individual plates, spoon the sauce over them, sprinkle with the remaining basil, and serve.

Sous Vide Pastrami Recipe

Time: 36 to 48 Hours
Temperature: 137°F / 57°C
Serves: 4

3-4 pounds short ribs, brisket, or other tough cut
4 english muffins, sliced
4 slices smoked gouda, or other smoked cheese

For the Coleslaw
½ head of cabbage, thinly sliced
4 to 8 carrots, julienned
½ cup red wine or sherry vinegar
1 shallot, diced
3 tablespoons mustard, preferably whole grained or dijon
1 ¼ cups olive oil

For the Brine
1 gallon water
1 ½ cups salt
1 cup sugar
8 teaspoons pink salt
1 tablespoon pickling spice
½ cup brown sugar
5 garlic cloves, minced
1 tablespoon coriander seeds
1 tablespoon black peppercorns

The process of making pastrami is surprisingly simple, especially considering how few people make their own. There are multiple steps in the process but each one is very easy. The brine and the idea for short rib pastrami is shamelessly adapted from Michael Ruhlman's Charcuterie[20] and his blog[21].

Once the sous vide pastrami is done cooking simply remove it from the pouches, slice and serve. You can use it however you normally like pastrami, I ate it on a toasted english muffin, topped with a mustard vinegar coleslaw, smoked gouda cheese, and mustard. I also served it with a light tomato, carrot, and cucumber salad to help cut the richness of the pastrami.

For breakfast the next day I mixed my leftovers with some diced potatoes, garlic, and poblano peppers in a pastrami hash topped with egg. The perfect leftovers breakfast!

Brining
To make the brine combine all the brine ingredients into a pot and bring to a boil. Reduce to a simmer for 5 minutes then remove from the heat and cool.

Once the brine is cool place the short rib meat in a non-reactive container large enough to hold it and cover with the brine. Place in the refrigerator for 2 to 3 days making sure the short rib meat stays submerged the entire time.

Smoking
Take your short ribs out of the brine and smoke them. There are three normal methods for adding smoke to the pastrami, use whichever method you prefer.

1) Use a smoker or grill with wood chips to smoke the short rib meat for a few hours before sous viding.

2) Grill the short rib meat quickly over on a hot grill to capture some smoke and charcoal flavor.

3) When sealing the short rib pastrami in the sous vide pouch add Liquid Smoke to it.

Once you have added the smoke to your short rib meat preheat your sous vide water bath to 137°F.

Seal the short ribs in a sous vide pouch and place the pouch into your water bath. Let it cook for 36 to 48 hours.

Finishing

About 45 minutes before you are ready to eat begin to prepare the coleslaw. Mix together the cabbage and carrots. In a separate bowl mix together the mustard, vinegar, shallot, salt, and pepper. Slowly whisk in the olive oil until it has formed a vinaigrette. Pour on top of the cabbage and carrots and mix together.

Remove the sous vide short rib pastrami from the sous vide pouch and slice roughly.

Toast the english muffins. Add the smoked gouda to the bottom half of the english muffin and toast until the cheese has melted.

Top with the pastrami and coleslaw and enjoy!

BBQ Beef

Time: 36 to 48 Hours
Temperature: 131°F / 55°C
Serves: 4 to 8

3 pound Top Round Roast, cut into 1 ½" slabs
2-4 sprigs rosemary
⅔ cup BBQ sauce
Salt and pepper

This recipe shows a good way to take an inexpensive and tough cut of meat and turn it into tender steaks. Here we add BBQ sauce for extra flavor but you can use any seasonings you prefer.

Pre-Bath
Preheat the water bath to 131°F / 55°C.

Salt and pepper the meat then add it to the sous vide pouches. Place the rosemary sprigs and ½ of the BBQ sauce in the pouches and then seal. Place in the water bath for 36 to 48 hours. For a grass-fed roast 12 to 24 hours should be good.

Finishing
Preheat a grill to very hot.

Take the beef slabs out of the water bath and remove them from the pouches. Pat them dry with a paper towel or dish cloth. Quickly sear the slabs on the grill for 1 to 2 minutes per side. Brush both sides with the BBQ sauce and grill for 30 seconds on each side.

Take the beef off the grill and serve as you would a steak. It is great with mashed potatoes or french fries and roasted broccoli.

Beef Stew

Time: 12 to 24 Hours
Temperature: 135°F / 57.2°C
Serves: 4

For the Meat
1 ½ to 2 pounds stew meat or chuck roast cut into 1" chunks
½ teaspoon cumin powder
½ teaspoon coriander powder
1 teaspoon garlic powder
2 thyme sprigs
2 rosemary sprigs
Salt and pepper

For the Stew
2 tablespoons olive oil
1 onion, diced
5 carrots, peeled and cut into 1" pieces
12 ounces baby bella mushrooms, washed and quartered
4 fresh thyme sprigs
4 cups beef stock
¾ cup red wine
2 cups water
4 red potatoes, cut in half
½ cup fresh parsley, chopped
¼ cup fresh chives, chopped

This is a nice and hearty winter stew. It's also a great way to use up tough cuts of meat. The sous vide helps to tenderize the meat without making it so tender that it doesn't stand out in the stew.

Pre-Bath
Heat the water bath to 135°F / 57.2°C.

Mix the spices together in a small bowl. Salt and pepper the meat and then sprinkle the spices over the top. Add to sous vide pouches along with the thyme and rosemary. Seal the pouches and place in the water bath to cook for 12 to 24 hours.

Finishing
Start the stew about an hour before the meat will be done.

In a pot over medium heat add the olive oil and warm. Add the carrots and onion and cook until the onion begins to turn translucent. Add the mushrooms and cook for another few minutes. Add the thyme, stock, wine, water and potatoes and bring to a simmer. Cook uncovered about 30 minutes.

Take the beef out of the sous vide pouches and add to the stew along with the juices from the bag. Cook for another 5 minutes and then serve in individual bowls with slices of crusty bread on the side.

"Classic" Pot Roast

Time: 2 to 3 Days
Temperature: 137°F / 58.3°C
Serves: 4 to 8

For the Roast
3 pounds pot roast
3 rosemary sprigs
3 thyme sprigs
Salt and pepper

For the Gravy
1 cup beef or chicken stock
2 tablespoons flour
2 tablespoons cold water
4 tablespoons of butter, cut into slices

This recipes helps create a "classic" pot roast, just one that is incredibly tender. It is best when served with some roasted carrots and mashed potatoes.

Pre-Bath
Preheat the water bath to 137°F / 58.3°C.

Salt and pepper the roast and then place in the sous vide pouch. Add the herbs and seal the pouch. Place in the water bath for 2 to 3 days.

Finishing
Preheat a grill or pan to very hot.

Take the roast out of the water bath and remove it from the pouch, reserving the liquid. Pat it dry with a paper towel or dish cloth.

Place the reserved liquid into a pan with the stock and bring to a boil. Mix together the flour and cold water in a bowl and then whisk into the pan. Bring to a boil and then reduce the heat to medium-low.

Quickly sear the slabs on the grill or pan for 1 to 2 minutes per side.

While the meat is cooking stir the butter into the gravy a tablespoon at a time.

Take the roast off the grill, slice it and serve with the gravy on top or in a bowl on the side.

Beef Steaks and Tender Cuts

Using sous vide to cook steaks and other tender cuts of beef allows you to always cook it perfectly and there is nothing better than a perfectly cooked steak!

If you are interesting in staying up to date with the work we are doing in sous vide feel free to follow us on Twitter. We post articles we find interesting, links to new recipes, and other items of interest.

We are @jasonlogsdon_sv

Overview

There are two main benefits to cooking steaks and other tender cuts of beef with sous vide. The first benefit is that sous vide allows you to perfectly cook the steak every time. The other benefit is the ability to turn tougher, but more flavorful, steaks such as flank steak into very tender steaks through longer cooking times.

This is accomplished because cooking tough cuts of beef with sous vide allows you to break down and tenderize the meat without cooking it above medium-rare and drying it out. Once temperatures in beef go above 140°F the meat begins to dry out and become more bland, however, they also start to tenderize more quickly which is why tough roasts and braises are done for hours at high temperatures. Using sous vide, you can hold the meat below 140°F for a long enough time for the tenderizing process to run its course.

I often use steaks cooked with sous vide as a basis for many normal steak dishes, such as fajitas or steak salad. You can also just add a nice salsa or sauce to the top of the steak and eat it that way. You can use sous vide steak in any of your favorite recipes, simply replace the cooking step in the recipe with the already cooked sous vide steak and then continue the rest of the recipe.

Time and Temperature Guidelines

The FDA states that beef is safe when it is held at 130°F for over 112 minutes, or 140°F for over 12 minutes. This is very easy to do with sous vide and the main reason we recommend cooking most beef cuts medium-rare since beef is most tender at that temperature.

Additionally, the center of "whole" muscles are sterile but due to mechanical tenderization that some meat packagers use the muscles can be compromised. So unless you trust your supplier it is advisable to cook beef to at least 130°F throughout.

Medium-rare steak is cooked between 130°F to 139°F, we recommend cooking it at 131°F to give yourself a few degrees of temperature variation above the bottom of the safe zone but feel free to experiment with any temperatures in that range. Depending on the toughness of the cut of beef, it may need to be cooked anywhere from 2 hours up to 1 or 2 days.

For each steak we also give directions for medium, these are normally cooked between 140°F and 149°F, though we recommend not going above 140°F because the beef begins drying out quickly and with sous vide there is no gain in food safety above 131°F.

Most steaks can be cooked sous vide for 2 to 4 hours and will result in a more tender version of how that steak traditionally tastes. However, for some tougher steaks longer cooking times can result in steak with tenderness rivaling tenderloin with no loss of the full, beefy flavor these cuts are known for.

It is also good to keep in mind that meat of different quality cooks at different speeds. For instance, most grass fed beef cooks faster and needs less time to tenderize.

General Process

The normal method of cooking steak with sous vide is very simple.

First, preheat your sous vide machine to the temperature desired, we recommend 131°F to 140°F for most cuts.

Take the meat and sprinkle it with salt and pepper and seal it into a sous vide pouch. You can also season the meat before sealing it with any normal steak seasoning such as:

- Fresh or dried thyme or rosemary
- Spice powders such as onion, garlic, paprika, coriander, or cumin
- Chile powders like ancho, chipotle, cayenne
- Marinades, though you don't need much
- Sauces like A1, worcester sauce, BBQ sauce, etc.

If adding a sauce or marinade, make sure your vacuum sealer does not suck it out, you can normally seal it before all the air is out to prevent this. Also, be sure to go light with fresh garlic, onions, or ginger, as they can begin to take on a bad flavor over the longer cooking times.

After sealing the pouch place it into the water bath for the indicated cooking time.

Once it's fully cooked remove it from the pouch and pat it dry. At this point you can sear the meat in a hot skillet or grill it over high heat to add a nice crust to it.

Once the meat is done cooking you can use it as you would any regular steak including cutting it up for salad, slicing it for fajitas or just eating it plain. You can also make a nice gravy or pan sauce from the liquid leftover in the sous vide pouch.

Another very convenient use of sous vide is to use it to defrost and cook steaks that come straight from the freezer. As long as the steak is vacuum sealed in a suitable bag you can take it directly from the freezer and put it in a preheated water bath. Just add 15-30 minutes to the cooking time and it should come out perfectly.

Recipe Notes

Most of the cuts of steak used in these recipes are completely interchangeable. Just adjust the cooking time accordingly to match the type of steak you are using.

The cooking times are expressed in a wide range. The steaks will be tasty at the lower end of the range but will get more tender as you near the top of it. Choose the time that fits your schedule and your taste. For instance, I prefer my flank steaks to have more bite to them instead of being meltingly tender so I cook them for 5 to 10 hours instead of a 24 to 48.

Remember that grass-fed beef will often tenderize much faster than store bought steaks. If you are unsure about how fast it is becoming tender just open up the sous vide pouch and cut off a piece. If it's not tender enough you can always reseal it and cook it longer. If it is done and it's not time to eat just chill the steak in a ice bath and reheat it later.

Ancho Ribeye with Spicy Sweet Mint Glaze

Time: 2 to 8 Hours
Temperature: 131°F / 55°C
Serves: 2

For the Steak
1-1 ½ pounds ribeye steak
1 teaspoon ancho powder
½ teaspoon powdered thyme
Salt and pepper

For the Glaze
4 tablespoons mustard, preferably Dijon
1 ½ tablespoons bottled horseradish
6 mint leaves
3 tablespoons honey
Salt and pepper

These steaks combine the fruity-heat of ancho peppers with the sharp bite of horseradish and mustard. These flavors work great with ribeye steaks because the richness of the fat helps to cut the heat. They can also be used with other tender cuts of steak or even help spice up chicken breasts or pork chops. They are great when served with some pureed sweet potatoes or sweet corn on the cob.

Pre-Bath
Preheat the water bath to 131°F / 55°C.

Sprinkle the ancho powder and thyme on the steaks then salt and pepper them. Add to the sous vide pouches, seal and place in the water bath. Cook the steaks for 2 to 8 hours.

Finishing
Preheat a grill to high heat.

Whisk together all the glaze ingredients in a small bowl and set aside. Remove the steaks from the sous vide pouches and pat dry. Coat the steaks with the glaze and quickly grill for 1 to 2 minutes per side, brushing on more glaze when you turn them. Remove from the heat and serve.

Herb Crusted Rib Steak

Time: 2 to 8 Hours
Temperature: 131°F / 55°C
Serves: 2

For the Steak
1-1 ½ pounds rib steak, cut into two portions
Salt and pepper

For the Rub
¼ cup dried rosemary
1 tablespoon dried oregano
1 tablespoon dried basil
1 tablespoon dried parsley
1 tablespoon sage
1 tablespoon dried garlic flakes
¼ cup coarse salt (kosher or sea)
2 tablespoons cracked black pepper

The dried herbs in this rub help to add some nice depth of flavor to the meat. You can also sear these steaks in a hot pan if you prefer instead of grilling them. They pair nicely with a crisp green salad or even with a side of angle hair pasta with garlic and olive oil.

Pre-Bath
Preheat the water bath to 131°F / 55°C.

In a bowl mix together all of the ingredients for the rub. Sprinkle the rub on the steak then salt and pepper them. Add to the sous vide pouches, seal, and place in the water bath. Cook the steaks for 2 to 8 hours.

Finishing
Preheat a grill to high heat.

Remove the steaks from the sous vide pouch and pat dry. Quickly grill for 1 to 2 minutes per side, just until browned. Remove from the heat and serve.

Orange Beef

Time: 2 to 10 Hours
Temperature: 131°F / 55°C
Serves: 4

For the Steak
1 ½ pound sirloin steak
½ teaspoon ginger powder
1 teaspoon garlic powder
Salt and pepper

For the Sauce
2 oranges, washed and dried
3 scallions, thinly sliced
1 tablespoon fresh ginger, minced
1 tablespoon garlic, minced
4 tablespoons sesame oil
1 ½ cups orange juice
2 tablespoons soy sauce
2 tablespoons honey
Salt and pepper
½ tablespoon grated orange peel (optional)

The grated orange peel adds some flavor without overpowering it. You can use a microplane or the small holes on a grater. This dish is great when served over white or basmati rice. This recipe is also very good with chicken or pork and the sauce is excellent poured onto swordfish steaks. For an even fuller meal you can add steamed broccoli, snap peas, or other vegetables to it.

Pre-Bath
Preheat your sous vide water bath to 131°F / 55°C.

Sprinkle the spices on the steak and then salt and pepper it. Put it into the sous vide pouch and seal. Place the steaks into the water bath for 2 to 10 hours.

For the Sauce
About 20 minutes before the steaks are done start on the sauce.

Grate the skin and set aside. Remove the rest of the skin and the white pith then cut the orange into segments. Do this over a bowl so the juice is reserved.

Heat a pan over medium heat. Add the oil and scallions and cook for 2 to 3 minutes. Add the garlic and ginger and cook for 1 to 2 minutes. Add the orange juice, soy sauce, honey, and salt and pepper, and cook until thickened, about 5 to 10 minutes.

Finishing
Remove the steak from the sous vide bath and pat dry. Sear it over high heat on a grill or in a pan just until browned, 1 to 2 minutes per side. Remove from the heat and slice into bite-size pieces.

Stir the steak pieces and the orange segments into the orange sauce and heat through. You can also add some of the juices from the bag for extra beef flavor.

Put a spoonful of white rice on a plate and top with the beef and orange mixture. Sprinkle with the orange peel and serve.

Filet Mignon with Gorgonzola Sauce

Time: 2 to 4 Hours
Temperature: 131°F / 55°C
Serves: 4

For the Steak
4 portions of filet mignon, about 1 to 1 ½ pounds
4 thyme sprigs
2 rosemary sprigs
Salt and pepper

For the Blue Cheese
¼ cup gorgonzola cheese
2 tablespoons heavy cream
1 tablespoons lemon juice
4 tablespoons olive oil
Salt and pepper

Since filet mignon is normally a blander cut of meat it can normally use a pick-me-up. Blue cheese is a classic paring but here we go with gorgonzola. This sauce really helps to add some richness to the otherwise lean filet.

Pre-Bath
Preheat the water bath to 131°F / 55°C.

Salt and pepper the steaks then add to the sous vide pouches. Add the thyme and rosemary then seal and place in the water bath. Cook the steaks for 2 to 4 hours.

Finishing
To make the gorgonzola cheese sauce place all of the ingredients in a food processor and process until smooth.

Take the steaks out of the pouches and pat dry. Sear them on a very hot grill or in a hot pan, about 1 to 2 minutes per side. Place the steaks on a plate and spoon the blue cheese sauce over the top and serve.

Sirloin Steak with Spring Salsa

Time: 3 to 10 Hours
Temperature: 131°F / 55°C
Serves: 4

For the Steak
1 to 2 pounds sirloin steak
1 teaspoon dried thyme
1 teaspoon cumin powder
Salt and pepper

For the Salsa
1 cup cherry tomatoes, halved
1 cup corn kernels, cooked
¼ red onion, diced
¼ cup basil, diced
1 tablespoon white wine vinegar
1 tablespoon olive oil
Salt and pepper

This spring salsa is very simple to make and really adds some lightness and flavor to the dish. It's great in late spring when the cherry tomatoes are just starting to ripen.

Pre-Bath
Preheat the water bath to 131°F / 55°C.

Salt and pepper the steaks then add to the sous vide pouches. Add the cumin and dried thyme and then seal and place in the water bath. Cook the steaks for 2 to 8 hours.

Finishing
To make the salsa mix all of the ingredients in a bowl. It's best to make the salsa right before you take the steaks out of the water bath.

Take the steaks out of the pouches and pat dry. Sear them on a very hot grill or in a hot pan, about 1 to 2 minutes per side. Place the steaks on a plate and top with a spoonful or two of the salsa.

Ribeye Steak with Herb Butter

Time: 2 to 8 Hours
Temperature: 131°F / 55°C
Serves: 4

For the Steak
4 portions of ribeye steak, 1 ½ to 2 pounds total
1 teaspoon dried thyme
2 teaspoons garlic powder
Salt and pepper

For the Butter
½ stick butter, softened at room temperature
1 tablespoon fresh parsley, finely chopped
1 tablespoon fresh basil, finely chopped
1 tablespoon fresh tarragon, finely chopped
⅛ teaspoon ground black pepper

The herbs in this butter add some lightness to the dish while the butter adds great richness. You can substitute any of the herbs and try out other combinations you like.

Pre-Bath
Preheat the water bath to 131°F / 55°C.

Salt and pepper the steaks then add to the sous vide pouches. Add the garlic powder and dried thyme and then seal and place in the water bath. Cook the steaks for 2 to 8 hours.

Finishing
To make the butter place all of the butter ingredients in a bowl and mix and mash thoroughly using a fork.

Take the steaks out of the pouches and pat dry. Sear them on a very hot grill or in a hot pan, about 1 to 2 minutes per side. Place the steaks on a plate and top with a dollop or two of the butter.

Flank Steak with Tomatillo Salsa

Time: 2 to 12 Hours or 1 to 2 Days
Temperature: 131°F / 55°C
Serves: 4 to 6

For the Steak
1 to 2 pounds flank steak
1 teaspoon dried thyme
1 teaspoon cumin powder
Salt and pepper

For the Salsa
4 to 8 tomatillos, 1 to 2 cups, diced
1 cup corn kernels, cooked
½ cup cilantro, chopped
1 shallot, diced
1 tablespoon cider vinegar
1 tablespoon olive oil
Salt and pepper

I prefer my flank steak to have some bite to it so I normally cook it for 2 to 12 hours but some people prefer it to be meltingly tender and cook it for 1 to 2 days. The tomatillo salsa adds a nice tang to complement the beefiness of the flank steak while the corn adds a sweet undertone and a little crunch. This dish is complemented nicely by refried beans and yellow rice.

Pre-Bath
Preheat the water bath to 131°F / 55°C.

Salt and pepper the steak then add to the sous vide pouches. Add the cumin and dried thyme and then seal and place in the water bath. Cook the steak for 2 to 8 hours.

Finishing
To make the salsa mix all of the salsa ingredients in a bowl. It's best to make the salsa right before you take the steaks out of the water bath.

Take the steaks out of the pouches and pat dry. Sear them on a very hot grill or in a hot pan, about 1 to 2 minutes per side. Cut the steak into ¼" to ½" strips and place on a plate. Top with a spoonful or two of the salsa.

Steak Sandwich with Caramelized Balsamic Onions

Time: 2 to 8 Hours
Temperature: 131°F / 55°C
Serves: 4

1 ½ pounds ribeye steak, cut into serving
portions
½ teaspoon garlic powder
½ teaspoon onion powder
½ teaspoon ancho chile powder
Salt and pepper
1 onion, thickly sliced
1 tablespoon balsamic vinegar
4 sandwich rolls or buns
4 slices havarti cheese

These steak sandwiches are great with steak fries or
macaroni and cheese. Cooking them sous vide ensures
that the steak is nice and tender and easy to bite
through.

Pre-Bath

Preheat the water bath to 131°F / 55°C.

Mix the spices together in a bowl. Salt and
pepper the steaks then sprinkle with the
spice mixture. Seal in sous vide pouches,
place in the water bath and cook for 2 to 8
hours.

Finishing

Preheat the broiler on the oven.

Add some canola or olive oil to a pan set
over medium to heat and warm. Add the
onions and salt and pepper them. Cook until
they are soft, about 15 minutes. About 10
minutes into the process add the balsamic
vinegar and stir well.

Remove the steaks from the water bath and
pat dry. Sear the steaks on a hot grill or in a
hot pan, about 1 or 2 minutes per side.

Place the steak on a roasting sheet. Cover
the top of the steak with the onions and top
with the cheese. Place the buns on the sheet
with the cut side up. Place the whole
roasting sheet under the broiler until the
cheese melts and the buns begin to brown.

Remove the sheet from the oven, place the
steak on top of the buns and serve.

Ribeye with Poblano-Onion Salsa

Time: 2 to 8 Hours
Temperature: 131°F / 55°C
Serves: 4 to 6

For the Steak
1 to 2 pounds ribeye steak, cut into 4 to 6
portions
1 teaspoon dried thyme
1 teaspoon ground coriander
½ teaspoon ancho chile powder
Salt and pepper

For the Salsa
2 tablespoons canola oil
2 onions, thickly sliced
2 poblano peppers, sliced
4 garlic cloves, minced
½ cup chicken stock
¼ cup cilantro, chopped
Salt and pepper

The chicken stock helps add a deepness of flavor to the poblano-onion salsa. The poblano peppers also add a mild heat to the dish.

Pre-Bath
Preheat the water bath to 131°F / 55°C.

Salt and pepper the steaks and add them to the sous vide pouches. Add the coriander, ancho powder, and dried thyme and then seal and place in the water bath. Cook the steaks for 2 to 8 hours.

Finishing
Heat the oil in a pan over medium to medium-high heat. Add the onions and cook until they just begin to brown. Add the poblano peppers and cook until they soften. Stir in the garlic and chicken stock and cook until reduced, a few minutes. Stir in the cilantro and remove from the heat.

Take the steaks out of the pouches and pat dry. Sear them on a very hot grill or in a hot pan, about 1 to 2 minutes per side. Place the steaks on a plate and top with several spoonfuls of the poblano-onion salsa.

Steaks with Chimichurri Sauce

Time: 2 to 10 Hours
Temperature: 131°F / 55°C
Serves: 4 to 6

For the Steak
2 pounds sirloin steak, cut into serving portions
½ teaspoon onion powder
½ teaspoon garlic powder
Salt and pepper

For the Chimichurri Sauce
1 bunch parsley
9 garlic cloves
3 tablespoons onion, diced
5 tablespoons cider vinegar
4 tablespoons water
2 teaspoons dried oregano
1 teaspoon hot pepper flakes, or to taste
Salt and pepper
1 cup olive oil

These Argentinian inspired steaks take advantage of the garlicky chimichurri sauce and are excellent when served with chunky mashed potatoes or rice. The chimichurri sauce also works great with chicken or pork.

Pre-Bath
Preheat the water bath to 131°F / 55°C.

Sprinkle the onion powder and garlic powder on the steaks then salt and pepper them. Add to the sous vide pouches, seal and place in the water bath. Cook the steaks for 2 to 10 hours.

For the Chimichurri Sauce
Put the parsley and garlic in a food processor and process until finely chopped. Add the rest of the ingredients, except for the olive oil, and process until lightly mixed. Add the oil in a thin stream while processing until the sauce comes together.

Finishing
Take the steaks out of the pouches and pat dry. Sear them on a very hot grill or in a hot pan, about 1 to 2 minutes per side. Place the steaks on a plate and spoon the chimichurri sauce over the top.

Steak Salad with Honey Mustard Dressing

Time: 2 to 10 Hours
Temperature: 131°F / 55°C
Serves: 2

For the Steak
1 pound sirloin steak
¼ teaspoon thyme powder
½ teaspoon garlic powder
Salt and pepper

For the Salad
½ red bell pepper, diced
4 baby bella or white button mushrooms, sliced
½ tomato, diced
Mixed greens or the lettuce of your choice

For the Dressing
3 tablespoons mayonnaise
1 tablespoon dijon mustard
1 tablespoon honey
Olive oil
Salt and pepper

This hearty steak salad calls for a honey mustard dressing but is equally good with any other flavorful dressing like blue cheese or thousand island. The steak can also be seared after being removed from the water bath to add additional flavor.

Pre-Bath
Preheat the water bath to 131°F / 55°C.

Prepare the meat by trimming off any excess fat. Dust the steak with the garlic powder and thyme powder. Salt and pepper the meat then seal it and place in the water bath. Let it cook for 2 to 10 hours.

Finishing
Make the dressing by whisking together the mayonnaise, dijon mustard, and honey. When it's combined slowly whisk in enough olive oil to mellow the flavor of the dressing to your taste. You can also add more honey or dijon to tweak the honey mustard dressing so it's the way you like it.

Assemble the salad by placing all the ingredients into a bowl or on a plate.

Remove the steak from the sous vide pouch and slice into short strips. Drizzle the honey mustard dressing on the salad and add the strips of the sous vide strip steak to it. Lightly sprinkle the salad with salt and pepper and serve.

Hassle Free Freezer Steaks

Time: 2 to 4 Hours
Temperature: 131°F / 55°C
Serves: 4

2 pounds of steak, cut ½ - 2 inches thick,
seasoned, sealed and frozen
½ teaspoon garlic powder
¼ teaspoon thyme powder
or seasonings of your choice

One of the most convenient uses of sous vide cooking is to use it to defrost and cook foods that come straight from the freezer. As long as the food is sealed you can take it directly from the freezer and put it in a preheated water bath. Just add 15-30 minutes to the recommended cooking time and it should come out perfectly.

You can use this method for any quick cooking sous vide meats like chicken breasts, pork chops, or steak. It's definitely a time saver and if you plan ahead you can save money by buying your meat in bulk and preparing it ahead of time.

Pre-Bath

There are two ways to prepare the steaks. You can either season them, seal them, then freeze them. You can do this step several months in advance.

The other option is to take previously frozen steaks and put them into a vacuum pouch while still frozen with the seasonings and seal them.

Preheat your sous vide water bath to 131°F / 55°C. Once the sous vide water is preheated put the steaks into the water and cook for 2 to 4 hours.

Finishing

Take the steaks out of the pouches and pat dry. Sear the sous vide steaks on a very hot grill or pan, until just browned, 1 to 2 minutes. Remove from the heat and serve.

Garlic-Basil Steak

Time: 1 to 2 Days
Temperature: 131°F / 55°C
Serves: 4

2 pounds top round steak, cut into serving portions
1 teaspoon garlic powder
1 teaspoon dried basil
1 teaspoon ground cumin
Salt and pepper

This recipe takes a tough cut of meat and tenderizes it nicely. It is great when served with roasted potatoes, asparagus, or a light salad. You can also try different spice combinations to see what you like best.

Pre-Bath
Preheat your sous vide water bath to 131°F / 55°C.

Sprinkle the garlic powder, cumin, and basil on the steak and then salt and pepper it. Place it into the sous vide pouch and seal it. Put into the the water bath and cook for 1 to 2 days.

Finishing
Take the steaks out of the pouches and pat dry. Sear the steaks on a very hot grill or pan, until just browned, 1 to 2 minutes per side. Remove from the heat and serve.

Spicy Chipotle Ribeye

Time: 2 to 8 Hours
Temperature: 131°F / 55°C
Serves: 4

2 pounds of ribeye, cut into serving portions
¼ teaspoon chipotle powder, or more to taste
1 teaspoon garlic powder
1 teaspoon paprika powder
Salt and pepper

These spicy and smoky ribeye steaks are great when served with mashed potatoes, macaroni and cheese, or macaroni salad.

Pre-Bath

Preheat your sous vide water bath to 131°F / 55°C.

Sprinkle the spices on the ribeye and then salt and pepper it. Place it into the sous vide pouch and seal it. Place into the water bath and cook for 2 to 8 hours.

Finishing

About 15 minutes before taking the steaks out of the sous vide preheat a grill or pan until very hot.

Take the steaks out of the pouches and pat dry. Sear the sous vide steaks on a very hot grill or pan, until just browned, 1 to 2 minutes. Remove from the heat and serve.

Flank Steak with Sauteed Mushrooms and Onions

Time: 2 to 12 Hours or 1 to 2 Days
Temperature: 131°F / 55°C
Serves: 4 to 6

For the Steak
1 to 2 pounds flank steak
1 teaspoon dried thyme
1 teaspoon ground coriander
½ teaspoon ancho chile powder
Salt and pepper

For the Onions
2 tablespoons canola oil
2 onions, thickly sliced
2 tablespoons butter
12 ounces baby bella mushrooms, thickly sliced
2 tablespoons balsamic vinegar
¼ cup basil, chopped
Salt and pepper

I prefer my flank steak to have some bite to it so I normally cook it for 2 to 12 hours but some people prefer it to be meltingly tender and cook it for 1 to 2 days. The balsamic vinegar helps add a nice tang and sweetness to the onions without overpowering their flavor. The flank steak has a very beefy flavor that is complemented by the onions and mushrooms. I prefer to use baby bella mushrooms but white button mushrooms will work fine as well.

Pre-Bath
Preheat the water bath to 131°F / 55°C.

Salt and pepper the steaks then add to the sous vide pouches. Add the coriander, ancho powder, and dried thyme and then seal and place in the water bath. Cook the steaks for 2 to 8 hours.

Finishing
Heat the oil in a pan over medium to medium-high heat. Add the onions and cook until they just begin to brown. Add the butter and the mushrooms and cook until they soften. Add the vinegar and stir while it reduces. Stir in the basil and remove from the heat.

Take the steaks out of the pouches and pat dry with a paper towel or dish towel. Sear them on a very hot grill or in a hot pan, about 1 to 2 minutes per side. Place the steaks on a plate and top with several spoonfuls of the mushrooms and onions.

Rosemary-Garlic Sirloin Steak

Time: 3 to 10 Hours
Temperature: 131°F / 55°C
Serves: 4

For the Steak
4 portions of sirloin steak, about 1 to 1 ½ pounds total
1 teaspoon garlic powder
2 rosemary sprigs
Salt and pepper

For the Butter
½ stick butter, softened at room temperature
3 garlic cloves, finely minced
1 tablespoon fresh rosemary, minced
⅛ teaspoon ground black pepper

This butter topping helps add great richness to the steak and imparts some more flavor, especially a sharp bite from the garlic. If there is leftover butter you can refrigerate it for several days or store it in the freezer for up to a month.

Pre-Bath
Preheat the water bath to 131°F / 55°C.

Salt and pepper the steaks then add to the sous vide pouches. Add the garlic powder and rosemary and then seal and place in the water bath. Cook the steaks for 3 to 10 hours.

Finishing
To make the butter place all of the butter ingredients in a bowl and mix and mash thoroughly using a fork.

Take the steaks out of the pouches and pat dry. Sear them on a very hot grill or in a hot pan, about 1 to 2 minutes per side. Place the steaks on a plate and top with a dollop or two of the butter.

Chicken and Eggs

Overcooked, bland, and dried out chicken is a common cooking stereotype for a reason. With practice it is possible to cook chicken perfectly using traditional methods but it is always a fine line between perfect and overcooked. Using sous vide always results in uniformly tender chicken that is very moist.

I often use sous vide chicken as a basis for other dishes such as chicken marsala, chicken parmigiana, fried chicken, and other chicken dishes with a coating. Fully cooking the chicken sous vide first, then applying and cooking the coating removes the guess work of trying to ensure the chicken is cooked through at the exact moment the coating turns nice and crispy.

Time and Temperature Guidelines

Chicken Meat

The FDA states that chicken is safe when it is held at 136°F for over 63 minutes, or 140°F for over 30 minutes. This is very easy to do with sous vide and almost impossible to do with traditional methods.

However, even though it is possible to cook chicken at temperatures below 140°F we have found that the texture is very different and tastes "raw". To avoid this we recommend chicken breasts cooked at 147°F for 1 to 4 hours and legs or thighs cooked at 147°F for 2 to 5 hours.

Chicken Eggs

As with traditional methods, the temperature used for sous vide chicken eggs depends on what type of egg you want. In general 135°F is "raw" but pasteurized and 158°F is very hard boiled. Most people feel the temperature for the perfect egg is 148°F and an equivalent of a poached egg is 142°F. Feel free to experiment in that range to see what you prefer. Sometimes people will take an egg that was cooked sous vide and place it directly into boiling water for 2 to 5 minutes to help solidify the white without cooking the yolk further.

Basic Process

Sous vide chicken is one of the easiest and fastest applications of sous vide cooking that there is. There are two different approaches, one for the chicken meat and another for the eggs.

Chicken Meat

Preheat your sous vide machine to the temperature desired, we recommend 147°F for most cuts but feel free to experiment within the safety guidelines above 136°F.

Seal the meat in a sous vide pouch with salt and pepper and other spices such as rosemary, sage, thyme, butter, or other seasonings you like. Place the sealed pouch into the water bath for the indicated cooking time.

Once it's fully cooked remove it from the pouch and pat dry. At this point you can use the pre-cooked chicken in any number of typical chicken preparations. You can coat the chicken breast with flour and quickly deep fry it for moist fried chicken. You can cover it with a spice rub and quickly pan fry it for a great blackened chicken to use on a caesar salad or with beans and rice. Or you can just throw it on the grill for a minute on each side and brush BBQ sauce on it for a great BBQ chicken.

Chicken Skin

Due to the moisture present in sous vide cooking chicken skin that was in the pouch will not become crispy when cooked. The best solution is to take it off of the bird before cooking the meat sous vide.

As you get close to serving time, you can manually crisp the chicken skin. There are many methods that work, using a hot skillet with a little oil is normally quick. You can also brown it on a baking sheet in the oven set to 375°F but make sure you use one with raised edges to prevent fat from falling into the oven.

Chicken Eggs

Cooking sous vide chicken eggs is also very simple. Just preheat your water bath to the desired temperature, from 135°F for "raw" to 158°F for very hard boiled. Most people feel the temperature for the perfect egg is 148°F and an equivalent of a poached egg is 142°F.

Once you determine your temperature preference you place the egg, still in its shell, into the water bath for 45-60 minutes, or up to 2 hours. Once the time has passed you take the egg out and serve it as you would a normal soft or hard boiled egg.

Buttermilk Fried Chicken

Time: 2 to 4 Hours
Temperature: 141°F / 60.5°C
Serves: 4

4 chicken breasts
4 lemon slices
4 sage leaves
3 cups flour
2 tablespoons garlic powder
2 tablespoons paprika
1 teaspoon chipotle or cayenne powder
3 cups buttermilk
Canola oil for frying

One of the biggest issues with making fried chicken is trying to make sure the chicken is cooked through at the same time the crust is done. Using sous vide to cook the chicken first allows you to focus solely on the crust. These fried chicken breasts are great with fresh corn, mashed potatoes, or even macaroni and cheese.

Pre-Bath
Preheat the water bath to 141°F / 60.5°C.

Place each chicken breast in a pouch with a sage leaf and a lemon slice. Salt and pepper the chicken breasts and then seal them. Cook the chicken breasts for 2 to 4 hours.

Finishing
Near the end of the cooking time, set up the batter stations and the oil.

Combine the flour, garlic powder, paprika, and chipotle powder into a shallow dish and mix thoroughly. Pour the buttermilk into a separate shallow dish. Fill a deep pot with canola oil to a depth of around 3" and heat to 365°F to 375°F, or use a deep-fryer if you have one. Be sure the oil fills the pot less than halfway since it will expand when the chicken breasts are added.

Remove the pouches from the water bath and take the chicken breasts out and pat each one dry with a paper towel. One at a time take each breast and dredge them in the flour mixture, then dip it in the buttermilk, and finally dredge it in the flour one more time. Set aside on a plate and repeat for all the chicken breasts.

Add the chicken breasts slowly, one at a time, into the hot oil and cook until the coating is browned and very crunchy. Remove from the oil, sprinkle with salt and pepper, and drain on a wire rack. Once all the chicken is cooked, serve.

Blackened Cajun Chicken

Time: 2 to 4 Hours
Temperature: 141°F / 60.5°C
Serves: 6

6 chicken breasts

For the Rub
½ cup coarse salt (kosher or sea)
2 tablespoons freshly ground black pepper
¼ cup paprika
2 tablespoons garlic powder
1½ tablespoons onion powder
1 tablespoon cayenne pepper, or to taste
1 tablespoon dried thyme
1 teaspoon freshly ground white pepper
1 teaspoon ground bay leaf

This is a traditional blackening rub that adds a spicy and flavorful kick to sometimes bland chicken breasts. It is very good when served with traditional sides like collard greens, coleslaw, and macaroni salad.

For the Rub

For the rub combine all the ingredients in a bowl and stir or whisk to mix. Any left over rub can be stored in a jar or tupperware container for several months in a cabinet.

Pre-Bath

Preheat the water bath to 141°F / 60.5°C.

Sprinkle the chicken breasts on both sides with the rub, place in the sous vide pouches and seal. Place the pouches into the water bath and cook for 2 to 4 hours.

Finishing

Heat a grill to high-heat. You won't be cooking the chicken long on it, just searing them, so use the hottest setting.

Remove the chicken from the pouch and blot dry with a paper towel. Place on the grill and cook for 1 to 2 minutes on each side. Remove from the heat and serve.

Chicken Mole

Time: 2 to 4 Hours
Temperature: 141°F / 60.5°C
Serves: 8

For the Chicken
8 chicken breasts
Salt and pepper

For the Mole
8 assorted medium-heat dried chile peppers such
as ancho, mulato, and pasilla
1 to 2 dried chipotle chilies
1 onion, coarsely chopped
4 garlic cloves, peeled
4 plum or roma tomatoes
3 tablespoons slivered almonds
2 tablespoons sesame seeds
½ teaspoon black peppercorns
1 teaspoon coriander seeds
1 cinnamon stick
2 whole cloves
½ teaspoon aniseed or fennel seed
¼ cup fresh cilantro, chopped
1 ½ ounces golden raisins
2 cups chicken stock
¼ cup olive oil
1 to 2 ounces dark or unsweetened chocolate
1 tablespoon honey
1 tablespoon apple cider vinegar

*Mole is one of my favorite sauces, especially when
done right. This is a more traditional preparation than
the more mild and sweet versions found at chain
restaurants. This dish takes advantage of the different
chile flavors and is very bold and full flavored.*

*This mole is best served with some kind of rice or
bread to soak up the wonderful sauce. It is also very
good with chicken thighs whose richness stands up
well to the bold flavors. Just increase the temperature
to 148°F and cook for 2 to 5 hours. Pork shoulder can
also be used in the recipe. You can also use this mole
sauce on a mexican pizza instead of tomato sauce.*

Pre-Bath
Preheat the water bath to 141°F / 60.5°C.

Salt and pepper the chicken breasts then seal
in the sous vide pouches. Place in the water
bath and cook for 2 to 4 hours.

For the Mole Sauce
You can make the mole sauce while the
chicken is cooking or make it up to a week
ahead of time and refrigerate it.

Roast the chilies for 2 minutes per side in a
dry pan over medium-high heat until
fragrant. Set aside to cool.

On a sheet pan with sides roast the
tomatoes, onion, and garlic in an oven set at
400°F until the onions soften, 10 to 20
minutes. Set aside to cool.

Add the almonds, sesame seeds,
peppercorns, coriander, cinnamon, cloves,
and aniseed to a pan and toast over medium
heat until fragrant and just starting to
brown, about 2 minutes. Set aside to cool.
Once cool add them to a spice grinder or
food processor. Process to a fine powder.

Cut the roasted chilies in half and remove
the seeds and stems. Put them in enough hot
water to cover them. After 30 minutes drain
them.

In a food processor place the tomatoes,
onion, garlic, chilies, ground spices, cilantro,
and raisins. Process until it becomes a
smooth paste, adding water if it is too thick.

Heat the olive oil in a large saucepan with
high sides over medium heat. Add the puree
from the food processor and cook for 5

minutes, stirring constantly, until it thickens. Reduce the heat to medium low and add the chicken stock, chocolate, honey, vinegar, and salt and stir to combine. Simmer the sauce for 10 minutes while stirring occasionally until it becomes thick but still pourable.

Any excess mole will keep for about a week in the refrigerator.

Finishing

If the mole was made ahead of time then reheat it in a deep pan, otherwise, continue from the steps above.

Take the chicken from the sous vide pouches and add to the mole sauce. Toss to coat well.

Place a chicken breast on a plate and spoon mole sauce on top. It's best when served over rice or with tortilla shells.

Green Chicken Thigh Curry

Time: 2 to 5 Hours
Temperature: 148°F / 64.4°C
Serves: 4

For the Chicken
1 pound chicken thighs, cut into bite-sized chunks
1 teaspoon garlic powder
1 teaspoon onion powder
Salt and pepper

For the Curry
1 tablespoon oil
1 onion, chopped
2 garlic cloves, minced
1 teaspoon ground cumin
2 tablespoons green curry paste
1½ cups coconut milk
½ cup water
½ cup green beans, cut into short pieces
1 tablespoon fish sauce
1 ½ tablespoons lime juice
1 tablespoon honey
¼ cup cilantro leaves

This green curry has a balance of heat and sweetness. You can add more or less curry paste to adjust the heat. I normally serve this with a pile of white rice on the side to absorb a lot of the sauce.

Pre-Bath
Preheat the water bath to 148°F / 64.4°C.

Sprinkle the chicken thighs with the garlic powder, onion powder, and salt and pepper. Place in the sous vide pouches and seal. Put in the water bath and cook for 2 to 5 hours.

For the Curry
Heat a pan over medium heat. Add the onion, garlic, ground cumin, and curry paste and stir constantly for about 1 minute. Add coconut milk and water and bring to a boil. Add the beans then turn down the heat and simmer for 10 minutes.

Just before serving stir in the fish sauce, lime juice, and honey.

Finishing
Take the chicken thighs out of the pouches and place in a serving dish. Pour the curry over the top and garnish with the cilantro leaves. Serve alongside white or fried rice and with crusty bread or na'an for soaking up the curry.

Spicy Chicken Caesar Salad

Time: 2 to 4 Hours
Temperature: 141°F / 60.5°C
Serves: 6

For the Chicken
2 to 3 chicken breasts
1 teaspoon garlic powder
½ teaspoon ground coriander
¼ teaspoon ground ancho pepper
Salt and pepper

1 head romaine lettuce, coarsely chopped
2 cups croutons
½ cup parmesan cheese, freshly grated

For the Dressing
½ to 1 chipotle pepper in adobo sauce
1 egg yolk
2 anchovy filets
1 teaspoon Dijon mustard
1 teaspoon minced garlic
3 tablespoons fresh lemon juice
½ cup olive oil
Salt and pepper

The chipotle pepper adds a nice kick to the classic caesar dressing. You can add the chipotle pepper slowly to the dressing to make sure it's not too spicy for you. To make your own fresh croutons you can see the Pesto Turkey Breast Salad recipe.

Pre-Bath
Preheat the water bath to 141°F / 60.5°C.

In a small bowl mix together the spices. Season the chicken breasts with the salt and pepper then sprinkle with the spices. Add to the sous vide pouch and seal.

Place the sous vide pouch into the water bath and cook for 2 to 4 hours.

Finishing
First, make the dressing. Place the egg yolks, anchovies, garlic, mustard, chipotle pepper and lemon juice into a food processor and process until thoroughly mixed. With the food processor still running slowly add the oil. Add salt and pepper, tasting until the seasoning is right.

Take the chicken out of the pouch and pat dry. Sear the chicken over high-heat in a hot pan until just browned, about 1 to 2 minutes per side. Remove from the heat and slice.

Place the lettuce in a large bowl. Add enough dressing to coat and toss the lettuce to evenly mix. Place the coated lettuce on individual plates. Top with the chicken, parmesan cheese, and croutons. Crack some fresh pepper on top and serve.

Chicken with Sauteed Peppers and Onion

Time: 2 to 4 Hours
Temperature: 141°F / 60.5°C
Serves: 6

For the Chicken
6 chicken breasts
1 teaspoon dried thyme
1 teaspoon cumin powder
1 teaspoon coriander powder
Salt and pepper

For the Peppers and Onions
2 tablespoons canola oil
2 onions, thickly sliced
2 red bell peppers, sliced
4 garlic cloves, minced
½ cup chicken stock
¼ cup parsley, chopped
Salt and pepper

The chicken stock adds a lot of depth and richness to the peppers and onions, it also helps to cut the sweetness of the red peppers. The pepper and onions really up the flavor of the sometimes bland chicken breasts.

Pre-Bath
Preheat the water bath to 141°F / 60.5°C.

Salt and pepper the chicken breasts then add to the sous vide pouches. Add the cumin, thyme, and coriander and then seal and place in the water bath. Cook the chicken for 2 to 4 hours.

Finishing
Heat the oil in a pan over medium to medium-high heat. Add the onions and cook until they just begin to brown. Add the red peppers and cook until they soften. Stir in the garlic and chicken stock and cook until reduced, a few minutes. Stir in the parsley and remove from the heat.

Take the chicken out of the pouches and pat dry. Sear them on a very hot grill or in a hot pan, about 1 to 2 minutes per side. Place the chicken on a plate and top with several spoonfuls of the peppers and onions.

BBQ Chicken Thighs

Time: 2 to 5 Hours
Temperature: 148°F / 64.4°C
Serves: 4

6 chicken thighs
½ teaspoon pepper
1 tablespoon garlic powder
3 sprigs of thyme
1-2 cups BBQ sauce
Salt and pepper

These chicken thighs are very quick to put together and have great flavor, especially if you have a good BBQ sauce. They pair well with watermelon, green beans, or wild rice.

Pre-Bath
Preheat the water bath to 148°F / 64.4°C.

Trim most of the excess fat off of the thighs. Evenly distribute the garlic powder over them, then salt and pepper each one. Place the chicken thighs in the pouches with one half of a thyme sprig per thigh then seal them. Cook the chicken thighs for 2 to 5 hours.

Finishing
Heat a grill to high-heat. You won't be cooking the thighs long on it, just searing them, so use the hottest setting.

Remove the thighs from the pouch, blot dry with a paper towel, and place on a plate. Smear a light layer of the BBQ sauce on the thighs then place on the grill and cook for 1 to 2 minutes, until the sauce starts to blacken and the thighs have a good sear on them.

Remove the thighs from the grill, smear another light layer of BBQ sauce on them and serve with the rest of the sauce on the side.

Chicken Sandwich with Sauteed Mushrooms

Time: 2 to 4 Hours
Temperature: 145°F / 62.7°C
Serves: 4

4 chicken breasts
½ teaspoon paprika
½ teaspoon garlic powder
½ teaspoon onion powder
Salt and pepper
½ onion, thickly sliced
10 mushrooms, thickly sliced
4 hamburger buns or rolls
4 slices provolone cheese
4 dill pickles

These chicken burgers are great with the normal accompaniments for a burger such as chips or fries and potato salad. For a healthier meal you can eat it with a side of steamed veggies or a side salad.

Pre-Bath
Preheat the water bath to 145°F / 62.7°C.

Mix the spices together in a bowl. Salt and pepper the chicken breasts then sprinkle with the spice mixture. Seal in sous vide pouches, place in the water bath and cook for 2 to 4 hours.

Finishing
Preheat the broiler on the oven.

Add some canola or olive oil to a pan set over medium heat and warm. Add the onions and mushrooms, stirring occasionally, until they are soft, about 10 minutes.

Remove the chicken breasts from the water bath and pat dry. Place the chicken on a roasting sheet. Cover the top of the chicken with the onions and mushrooms mixture and top with the cheese. Place the buns on the sheet with the cut side up. Place the whole roasting sheet under the broiler until the cheese melts and the buns begin to brown.

Remove the sheet from the oven, place the chicken on top of the buns and serve with the dill pickles.

Jamaican Jerk Chicken Thighs

Time: 2 to 5 Hours
Temperature: 148°F / 64.4°C
Serves: 8

2 to 3 pounds of chicken thighs

For the Jerk Paste
3 to 10 habanero or Scotch bonnet chilies,
stemmed and cut in half
1 onion, coarsely chopped
2 bunches scallions (white and green parts),
trimmed and coarsely chopped
5 garlic cloves, coarsely chopped
½ cup fresh parsley, coarsely chopped
½ cup fresh cilantro, chopped
2 teaspoons fresh ginger, chopped
2 tablespoons coarse salt
2 tablespoons fresh thyme
1 tablespoon ground allspice
½ teaspoon ground cinnamon
½ teaspoon freshly grated nutmeg
1 teaspoon freshly ground black pepper
¼ cup brown sugar
½ cup fresh lime juice
¼ cup olive oil
2 tablespoons soy sauce
¼ cup cold water, or as needed

*Chicken thighs stand up great to this traditional
Jamaican jerk flavoring but it can also be used on
breasts or even pork chops or pork shoulder. A side of
rice and beans or mashed plantains is a great
complement to this dish. Any leftover paste can be
stored in the refrigerator for about a week.*

For the Jerk Paste
Add all of the dry ingredients to a food
processor and process to a coarse paste. Add
the remaining liquid ingredients and process
until the paste becomes spreadable.

Pre-Bath
Preheat the water bath to 148°F / 64.4°C.

Smear the chicken thighs all over with the
jerk paste. Add the thighs to the sous vide
pouches, seal, and place in the water bath.
Cook for 2 to 5 hours.

Finishing
Preheat a pan or grill to high heat.

Take the thighs out of the sous vide pouches
and pat dry. Cook them at high heat for 1 to
2 minutes per side. Remove from the heat
and serve.

Scrambled Eggs

Time: 18 Minutes
Temperature: 167°F / 75°C
Serves: 2

4 eggs
2 tablespoons unsalted butter
2 tablespoons heavy cream
3 strips of bacon, cut into lardons
Salt and pepper
1 tablespoon basil, cut into strips
Parmesan cheese for grating

Sous vide scrambled eggs are one of the more interesting dishes to cook. The resulting texture is much more like a custard than the often rubbery scrambled eggs we're used to here in America.

Here we use bacon lardons and basil chiffonade for garnish, along with some freshly grated parmesan cheese. It's wonderful when served with a fresh baguette or toast. And actually preparing the scrambled eggs couldn't be easier.

Pre-Bath

Preheat your sous vide setup to 167°F / 75°C.

To make the scrambled egg mixture beat together the eggs, cream, salt and pepper until mixed well. Grate a few tablespoons of the cheese into the scrambled egg mixture then pour the mixture into a sous vide pouch and add the butter.

Seal the pouch lightly, shutting off the vacuum when the eggs get close to the opening. A good way to help with this is to hang the sous vide pouch off the edge of your counter when sealing it.

Add the pouch with the scrambled eggs to the water bath. You will be initially cooking it for around 10 minutes.

Finishing

While the scrambled eggs are cooking, cook the bacon in a skillet over medium heat until crispy.

After 10 minutes take the egg pouch out of the water and massage it to break up the eggs. Return it to the water bath and cook for another 5-8 minutes, until the mixture begins to firm up.

Remove the sous vide pouch from the water and massage it once more. Then pour the sous vide scrambled eggs evenly into two bowls. Taste for seasonings and add any salt or pepper if needed. Add the cooked bacon lardons and basil chiffonade to the bowls. Then grate some parmesan cheese over the top and serve.

Spinach Salad with Soft "Boiled" Eggs

Time: 50 to 60 Minutes
Temperature: 147°F / 64°C
Serves: 4

4 eggs
4 bacon slices, cut across into thin strips
1 onion, sliced
3 garlic cloves, coarsely chopped
2 tablespoons honey
1 tablespoon balsamic vinegar
1 tablespoon olive oil
1 bag baby spinach
1 tomato, diced
Fresh parmesan cheese
Salt and pepper

The eggs, especially the yolks, add a ton of flavor to this salad. They go great with the bacon and cheese. Cooking the eggs sous vide allows you to accurately determine how hard or soft you would like them. Moving a few degrees in either direction results in dramatic changes.

Pre-Bath

Preheat the water bath to 147°F / 64°C.

Place the eggs, in the shell, directly into the water bath and cook for 50 to 60 minutes.

Finishing

While the eggs are cooking put together the rest of the salad, try to time the wilting of the spinach at the end of the recipe with when the eggs are done, 50 to 60 minutes after they went into the water bath.

Saute the bacon strips in large pan and cook for 5 to 6 minutes over medium heat to render the fat. Remove the bacon and set it aside. Pour out half the bacon fat and discard, leaving the rest in the pan.

Add the onion and garlic to the pan and cook until the onion turns soft. Add the honey and vinegar and cook until the onion begins to caramelize, 5 to 6 more minutes.

Add the spinach to the pan and stir until it is just wilted, about 1 minute. Remove from the heat and portion into 4 individual bowls. Top with the bacon and tomato.

Take the eggs out of the water bath using a slotted spoon or tongs. One at a time, gently crack the eggs on the counter and remove the top ¼ to ½ of the shell. At that point you should be able to turn the shell upside down and the egg should slide out. Add 1 sous vide egg to the top of each salad.

Drizzle some olive oil on each salad, grind some pepper on it and grate on the parmesan cheese to top it off before serving.

BBQ Chicken Breast

Time: 2 to 4 Hours
Temperature: 141°F / 60°C
Serves: 4

4 chicken breasts
1 or 2 sprigs of fresh thyme
1 or 2 sprigs of fresh rosemary
½ teaspoon ancho pepper, or more for a spicier chicken
Your Favorite BBQ Sauce

This sous vide chicken recipe will result in a fantastically moist BBQ chicken. It's also incredibly simple to do. The chicken goes great with some rice and a crispy salad, or macaroni and cheese and corn on the cob.

Pre-Bath

Preheat the water bath to 141°F / 60°C.

Lightly salt and pepper the chicken breast and place in a pouch. Add the thyme and rosemary and then seal. Place the chicken breasts in the water bath and cook for around 2 to 4 hours.

Finishing

Heat your grill to high temperature when you are getting close to serving the chicken.

Remove the sous vide chicken breasts from the pouch, pat them dry with a paper towel or dish cloth and coat the with BBQ sauce. Quickly grill the chicken breasts for 1 or 2 minutes per side, just enough time to develop some color. Remove from the heat and serve.

Lime-Curry Chicken Thighs

Time: 2 to 5 Hours
Temperature: 148°F / 64.4°C
Serves: 4

4 chicken thighs

For the Butter
½ cup unsalted butter, softened at room
temperature
1 lime, zest and juice
1 tablespoon honey
1 tablespoon red curry paste
½ teaspoon soy sauce
½ teaspoon rice wine or apple cider vinegar
Salt and pepper

¼ cup fresh cilantro, chopped, for garnish

The lime curry butter adds a rich, complex flavor to the already moist and tender chicken thighs.

Pre-Bath
Preheat the water bath to 148°F / 64.4°C.

Sprinkle salt and pepper on the chicken
thighs and place into the sous vide pouches.
Seal the pouches and place in the water bath
for 2 to 5 hours.

Finishing
About 10 minutes before the thighs are done
make the lime-curry butter. Add the red
curry paste, lime zest and juice, butter,
honey, vinegar, soy sauce, cilantro, and some
salt and pepper into a bowl. Mix together
thoroughly.

Take the chicken thighs out of the sous vide
pouches and pat dry. Sear over high heat in
a pan or on a grill. Put a chicken thigh on a
plate and place a spoonful of the lime-curry
butter on top and serve.

Chicken Marsala

Time: 2 to 4 Hours
Temperature: 141°F / 60°C
Serves: 4

4 chicken breasts
1 or 2 sprigs of fresh thyme
1 cup flour
3 cups of sliced mushrooms like baby bella, crimini, oyster, or porcini
¾ cup Marsala wine
¾ cup chicken stock
3 tablespoons butter
4 tablespoons chopped Italian parsley

Chicken Marsala is one of my favorite Italian dishes to make. It is such a simple recipe and is so easy to put together. Traditionally, the only tricky part is trying to make sure the chicken breasts are cooked through without turning them soggy. Using sous vide to pre-cook the chicken breasts eliminates this issue.

Using sous vide chicken breasts instead of the usual "pan-fry and simmer" method ensures that your chicken is cooked thoroughly and you can easily give them a nice crust with a quick sear over high heat. By eliminating the simmering at the end, the crust on the chicken stays nice and crisp and never becomes soggy.

Another benefit of using sous vide chicken is that you can use thicker breasts. Normally, when you make chicken marsala you pound the chicken into thin filets ¼ of an inch thick to ensure they cook thoroughly.

I prefer a little thicker and juicier chicken breast so I normally butterfly the breast and then cook it sous vide. It results in a more moist and hefty chicken marsala.

This dish goes well with a warm baguette and some angel hair pasta to soak up all the great sauce. Asparagus or steamed broccoli is also good.

Pre-Bath
Preheat the water bath to 141°F / 60°C.

Lightly salt and pepper the chicken breasts and place in a pouch with the thyme. Seal and place in the water bath and cook for 2 to 4 hours.

Finishing
Heat some oil in a saute pan over medium-high heat.

Remove the sous vide chicken breasts from the pouch, pat them dry with a paper towel or dish cloth. Dredge them in the flour and then quickly sear the chicken breasts for about 1 minute per side, just enough time to develop some color. Remove and place somewhere warm.

Add 1 tablespoon of butter to the pan and melt. Add the mushrooms to the pan and cook until they begin to brown and release their liquid, about 4 to 6 minutes.

Lower the heat to medium and add the Marsala wine to the pan. Simmer for about 1 minute to cook out the alcohol, scraping the bottom of the pan to dislodge the browned bits stuck there. Add the chicken stock to the pan. Let simmer for 5 to 10 minutes to reduce the sauce.

Put the sous vided and seared chicken breasts onto individual plates. Stir the remaining 2 tablespoons of butter into the sauce. Then spoon the mushrooms and marsala sauce evenly over the chicken breasts. Sprinkle the italian parsley over the top and serve.

Chicken Curry Salad

Time: 2 to 4 Hours
Temperature: 147°F / 63.8°C
Serves: 4

For the Chicken
4 chicken breasts
1 teaspoon garlic powder
1 teaspoon paprika powder
Salt and pepper

For the Salad
1 celery stalk, diced
2 carrots, peeled and diced
2 tablespoons fresh chives, chopped
2 tablespoons scallion, thinly sliced
⅛ cup fresh parsley, minced
⅛ cup fresh basil, minced
2 cups seedless grapes, halved
1 apple, preferably crisp and good for eating, peeled and diced
½ cup pecans, toasted

For the Dressing
2 teaspoons curry powder
2 tablespoons mayonnaise
⅓ cup fruit chutney
¼ cup olive oil
1 tablespoon lemon juice
½ teaspoon pepper
½ teaspoon salt

For added flavor you can sear the chicken after you take it out of the water bath. Feel free to experiment with the herbs and fruit in this salad. Pears would work well and tarragon would go great with tomatoes or fennel.

Pre-Bath
Preheat the water bath to 147°F / 63.8°C.

Salt and pepper the chicken breasts then sprinkle with the garlic and paprika powders. Seal in sous vide pouches, place in the water bath and cook for 2 to 4 hours.

Finishing
Take the chicken out of the water bath and chill in an ice-bath. While the chicken is cooling prepare the rest of the salad.

First make the dressing. In a large serving bowl whisk together all of the dressing ingredients. Add the celery, carrot, chives, scallion, parsley, basil, grapes, and apple and mix well.

Shred or chop the chicken into bite sizes pieces and add to the salad. Mix well and serve with the toasted nuts sprinkled on top.

Chicken Sandwich with Peppers and Onions

Time: 2 to 4 Hours
Temperature: 145°F / 62.7°C
Serves: 4

For the Chicken
4 chicken breasts
½ teaspoon garlic powder
½ teaspoon onion powder
½ teaspoon ancho powder
½ teaspoon dried thyme
Salt and pepper

1 onion, sliced into ¼" strips
½ red bell pepper, sliced into ¼" strips
½ orange bell pepper, sliced into ¼" strips
½ cup chicken stock
4 sandwich rolls or panini bread
4 slices fresh mozzarella cheese

These chicken sandwiches are very flavorful while still being very healthy. The bell peppers add a lot of flavor without overpowering the chicken. They go well with coleslaw and potato salad.

Pre-Bath
Preheat the water bath to 145°F / 62.7°C.

Mix the spices together in a bowl. Salt and pepper the chicken breasts then sprinkle with the spice mixture. Seal in sous vide pouches, place in the water bath and cook for 2 to 4 hours.

Finishing
Preheat the broiler on the oven.

Add some canola or olive oil to a pan set over medium heat and warm. Add the onions, salt and pepper them, and cook until they begin to soften, about 10 minutes. Add the bell peppers and cook for another 5 minutes. Add the chicken stock, mix well, and cook until it thickens.

Remove the chicken breasts from the water bath and pat dry. Place the chicken on a roasting sheet. Cover the chicken with the onions and pepper mixture and top with the cheese. Place the rolls on the sheet with the cut side up. Place the whole roasting sheet under the broiler until the cheese melts and the rolls begin to brown.

Remove the sheet from the oven, place the chicken on top of the rolls and serve.

Duck

There is nothing worse than overcooking a nice piece of duck. Luckily, sous vide makes perfect duck easy to achieve. Not only is it simple to cook perfectly tender and moist duck consistently but you can also confit duck very easily.

Sous vide duck is great when used as a basis for traditional duck dishes. And of course it is great plain with a pan sauce made from the liquids in the bag or with some olive oil.

We are constantly adding recipes to our website as we continue to experiment with sous vide. Maybe something there will inspire you.

You can find them at:
www.cookingsousvide.com/info/sous-vide-recipes

Time and Temperature Guidelines

The FDA states that duck is safe when it is held at 136°F for over 63 minutes, or 140°F for over 30 minutes. This is very easy to do with sous vide and almost impossible to do with traditional methods.

Duck breast is typically cooked medium-rare and we have found that 131°F for 2 to 4 hours works great. For standard duck legs or thighs we suggest 131°F for 2 to 4 hours.

If you are using the duck for shredding we have found cooking it to "Well" at 176°F for 8 to 10 hours results in still moist, fall-apart shredding duck.

Making duck confit is also very easy with sous vide and after being cured is cooked at 167°F for 10 to 20 hours with some duck fat in the pouch.

Basic Process

Cooking duck sous vide is very easy to do. It helps if the duck is no longer whole, as the smaller pieces will heat more quickly and evenly.

Preheat your sous vide machine to the temperature desired, we recommend 131°F

for most preparations but if you are using it for shredding or confit then a higher temperature is ideal.

Seal the meat in a sous vide pouch with salt and pepper and other spices such as rosemary, sage, thyme, butter, or any other seasonings you like with duck. Then place it into the water bath for the indicated cooking time.

Once it's fully cooked remove it from the pouch and pat dry. At this point you can sear the meat in a hot skillet to add a nice crust to it or you can slice it and serve as is. You can also make a great gravy or pan sauce from the liquids in the bag.

Duck skin that was in the pouch will not become crispy when cooked due to the moisture present in sous vide cooking. The best solution is to take it off of the bird before cooking the meat sous vide.

As you get close to serving time, you can manually crisp the duck skin. There are many methods that work, using a hot skillet with a little oil is normally quick and effective. You can also brown it on a baking sheet in the oven set to 375°F but make sure you use one with raised edges to prevent fat from falling into the oven.

Asian Duck Breast with Fried Rice

Time: 2 to 4 Hours
Temperature: 131°F / 55°C
Serves: 4

For the Duck
2 duck breasts
1 tablespoon Chinese 5-spice powder
½ tablespoon garlic powder
Salt and pepper

For the Fried Rice
2 tablespoons canola oil
1 leak, rinsed and cut into thin slices
3 carrots, julienned or thinly sliced
1 hot red chile, thinly sliced
1 tablespoon fresh ginger, grated
½ cup corn kernels, cooked
1 cup pineapple, diced
2 ⅓ cups cooked long grain rice
2 tablespoons soy sauce
1 tablespoon sherry vinegar
½ cup chicken stock

*This fried rice helps to add a nice base to enjoy this
Asian-inspired duck on. You can also add more
vegetables like broccoli, peas, or bok choy.*

Pre-Bath
Preheat the water bath to 131°F / 55°C.

Sprinkle the duck breasts with the Chinese
5-spice powder and garlic powder. Salt and
pepper them then add to the sous vide
pouches. Seal the pouches, place in the
water bath, and cook for 2 to 4 hours.

For the Rice
10 to 15 minutes before the duck is done
begin to make the rice.

In a pan over medium heat add the oil. Once
warmed add the leek and carrots and cook
for 5 to 10 minutes until the carrots begin to
soften. Add the pineapple, chile, ginger and
cook for 1 to 2 minutes.

Add the rice, pineapple, and corn and stir
well to mix. Stir in the soy sauce, sherry
vinegar, and stock and warm thoroughly.

Finishing
Remove the duck breasts from the sous vide
pouches and pat dry. In a very hot pan or on
a very hot grill sear the duck breasts on each
side, about 1 to 2 minutes each. Then cut the
duck breast into ¼" thick slices.

Place a spoonful of the rice onto a plate or in
a bowl. Lay several of the strips of duck on
top of each pile of rice and serve.

Apple and Duck Salad

Time: 2 to 4 Hours
Temperature: 131°F / 55°C
Serves: 4

For the Duck
2 duck breasts

For the Salad
1 apple, preferable a crisp, good eating variety,
quartered and thinly sliced
6 cups arugula or spinach, washed and dried
¼ cup pomegranate seeds
¼ cup sliced almonds, toasted
Feta cheese, crumbled

For the Vinaigrette
3 tablespoons cider vinegar
1 tablespoon honey
6 tablespoons olive oil
Salt and pepper

*Duck and apple goes well together and the vinaigrette
helps to cut the fattiness from the duck. Don't prep
the apples too far ahead of time or they will begin to
turn brown. You can also serve this with a fresh
baguette or hot rolls to round out the full meal.*

Pre-Bath
Preheat the water bath to 131°F / 55°C.

Sprinkle the duck breasts with the Chinese
5-spice powder and garlic powder. Salt and
pepper them then add to the sous vide
pouches. Seal the pouches then place in the
water bath and cook for 2 to 4 hours.

Finishing
Remove the duck breasts from the sous vide
pouches and pat dry.

Make the vinaigrette. Combine the vinegar,
honey, salt and pepper in a bowl. Then
slowly whisk in the olive oil.

In a very hot pan or on a very hot grill sear
the duck breasts on each side, about 1 to 2
minutes each. Then cut the duck breast meat
into ¼" thick slices.

Toss the arugula with enough dressing to
coat the leaves. Divide the arugula among 4
plates. Top with the apples and duck breast.
Add 1 tablespoon of pomegranate seeds to
each plate then top with the almonds and
feta cheese.

Sweet Licorice Duck Breasts

Time: 2 to 4 Hours
Temperature: 131°F / 55°C
Serves: 4

4 duck breasts
3 whole star anise
2 cinnamon sticks
3 tablespoons Sichuan peppercorns
2 tablespoons fennel seeds
1 teaspoon whole cloves

This recipe calls for freshly toasted and ground spices which adds a lot more depth and character than using pre-ground spices. However, if you don't have the time or inclination to do this it is still excellent with pre-ground spices, or even a pre-mixed 5-spice Chinese powder with some extra fennel seeds added.

Pre-Bath

In a pan set over medium-low heat add the spices and toast for 3 to 5 minutes until they become fragrant. Remove from the heat and once cooled grind them in a spice grinder.

Heat the water bath to 131°F / 55°C.

Rub the duck breasts with ¾ of the rub, reserving some to be used later. Seal the duck in the sous vide pouches and place into the water bath. Cook for 2 to 4 hours.

Finishing

Remove the duck from the sous vide pouches and pat dry. Cover 1 side with the spice rub and sear in a pan over high heat, about 1 to 2 minutes per side. Remove from the heat and serve.

Duck Salad with Orange Vinaigrette

Time: 2 to 4 Hours
Temperature: 131°F / 55°C
Serves: 4

4 duck breasts
1 cup orange juice
½ teaspoon mustard
2 tablespoons red wine vinegar
1 tablespoon honey
½ cup olive oil
Salt and pepper
Mixed greens
1 sweet red bell pepper, sliced
½ pint fresh raspberries or blackberries
½ cup pecans

The acid in the orange juice helps to cut the richness of the duck breast and the berries and bell pepper add a nice sweetness to it.

Pre-Bath

Heat the water bath to 131°F / 55°C.

Sprinkle the duck breasts with salt and pepper. Seal the duck in the sous vide pouches and place into the water bath. Cook for 2 to 4 hours.

Finishing

In a bowl mix together the orange juice, mustard, vinegar and honey. Whisk in the olive oil to create the vinaigrette.

Remove the duck from the sous vide pouches and pat dry. Sear in a pan over high heat, about 1 to 2 minutes per side. Remove from the heat and slice into ½″ slices.

To serve, place the greens in individual bowls or on plates. Top with the bell pepper and berries. Add the duck slices and spoon the vinaigrette on top. Add the pecans and serve.

Hot and Smoky Duck Legs

Time: 3 to 6 Hours
Temperature: 131°F / 55°C
Serves: 4

1 pound of duck legs
Salt and pepper

For the Marinade
3 roma tomatoes
4 garlic cloves, peeled
½ onion, coarsely chopped
½ cup lime juice
3 tablespoons orange juice
2 tablespoons apple cider or red wine vinegar
3 canned chipotle chilies in adobo sauce
1 teaspoon dried oregano
1 teaspoon salt
½ teaspoon ground cumin
½ teaspoon ground coriander
½ teaspoon black pepper

The rich duck legs hold up well to bolder flavors and here we pair chipotle chilies with citrus juices to complement them. You can add more or less chipotle chillies to your desired heat level.

For the Marinade

Put the tomatoes, onion, and garlic on a sheet pan with raised sides. Cook them in an oven set at 400°F until the onions soften, about 10 to 20 minutes. Set aside to cool.

Place the roasted vegetables and the remaining marinade ingredients into a blender and process into a thick puree.

Pre-Bath

Preheat the water bath to 131°F / 55°C.

Place the duck legs in a sous vide pouch and pour ½ the marinade over them. Reserve the rest of the marinade and place in the refrigerator. Seal duck and place in the water bath. Cook for 3 to 6 hours.

Finishing

Remove the duck legs from the sous vide pouches and pat dry. Sear them over high heat in a pan or on a grill until just browned, about 1 to 2 minutes. Serve with a spoonful of the reserved marinade on top.

Fish and Shellfish

Sous vide fish can be very flaky and moist and is cooked for only a short amount of time. The sous vide process cooks the fish without drying it out. Sous vide shellfish can be very tender and can avoid the toughness that can develop when they are overcooked with traditional methods.

Sous vide fish and shellfish is great when added to traditional seafood dishes such as seafood stews, chowders, or sandwiches. It is also great eaten plain with some olive oil and lemon juice or with a simple salsa of fresh vegetables.

Time and Temperature Guidelines

The FDA states that fish is safe when it is held at 135°F for over 27 minutes, or 140°F for over 8.65 minutes. This is very easy to do with sous vide.

We've found that in general the best tasting seafood is cooked at 132°F. However, unless it is cooked for over 45 minutes it is not fully pasteurized and should not be eaten if you have a weak immune system or the fish is of sushi-grade quality.

For fully pasteurized fish, it is best to cook them to 140°F. One note is that this will not kill any virus that are in the fish, but this is an issue with traditional methods as well.

General Process

The normal method of cooking seafood is about as simple as it gets.

Preheat your sous vide machine to the temperature desired, we recommend 132°F for most cuts unless you have sushi-grade fish and want to go lower.

For fish, take the fish and filet them and remove the skin and bones, or have your fish monger do it and just buy them as filets. For shellfish, remove any shell or non-edible parts.

Take the seafood and sprinkle it with salt and pepper and seal it into a sous vide pouch. You can also season the meat before sealing it with any normal seasoning such as:

- Fresh or dried thyme or rosemary
- Any spice powders such as onion, garlic, or paprika
- Lemon, lime, or orange zest
- Marinades, lemon juice, butter, or olive oil

If adding a sauce or marinade make sure your vacuum sealer does not suck it out, you can normally seal it before all the air is out to prevent this just fine. Also, we do not recommend using fresh garlic, onions, or ginger, as they can begin to take on a bad flavor.

After sealing the pouch place it into the water bath for the indicated cooking time.

Once it's fully cooked remove it from the pouch and pat dry. At this point you can sear the seafood in a hot skillet to add a nice crust to it or you can slice it and serve as is.

Once the seafood is done cooking you can use it as you would any typical cooked fish. Most seafood is great with some olive oil and a squeeze of lemon juice on it.

Recipe Notes

These recipes assume that the amount of fish requested is for portions of fish that are cleaned and deboned unless specified otherwise.

Simple Sous Vide Swordfish

Time: 15 to 30 Minutes
Temperature: 132°F / 55.5°C
Serves: 2

1 pound of swordfish, either chunks or a whole
filet
2 sprigs of thyme
½ to 1 tablespoon lemon verbena, diced
(optional)
1 teaspoon mint, diced
2 tablespoons butter
Salt and pepper

*Sous vide swordfish is exceptionally buttery and
tender. You can simply serve it with some blanched
green beans or a tomato-cucumber salad. If you sous
vide the whole swordfish filet you can quickly sear it
in a hot pan and serve it with rice or mashed potatoes
and a green salad. You could even rub some BBQ
sauce on it and throw it on the grill for a minute on
each side for a great BBQ swordfish dish.*

*Anyway you serve it, sous vide swordfish is a
meltingly tender main ingredient in any dish.*

Pre-Bath
Preheat the water bath to 132°F / 55.5°C.

Season the swordfish with the salt and
pepper then add to the sous vide pouch.
Add the thyme, lemon verbena, mint and
butter to the pouch and then seal.

Place the sous vide swordfish pouch into the
water bath for 15 to 30 minutes.

Finishing
Take the swordfish out of the pouch,
reserving the butter-herb liquid. If searing,
pat dry the swordfish and sear over high-
heat in a hot pan or on a hot grill. At that
point, simply plate with whatever sides you
decided on and serve.

I personally love the flavor of the butter-
herb liquid so I tend to use it as a sauce and
pour some over top of the swordfish.

Moroccan Snapper

Time: 10 to 30 Minutes
Temperature: 122°F / 50°C for sushi quality or
132°F / 55.6°C otherwise
Serves: 4

For the Fish
4 red snapper filets, cleaned
2 tablespoons butter or olive oil
Salt and pepper

For the Saffron-Citrus Sauce
1 lemon
1 grapefruit
1 lime
3 oranges
2 tablespoons canola or olive oil
1 yellow onion
1 zucchini, diced
1 teaspoon saffron threads
1 teaspoon diced chile pepper, serrano or
jalapeno works well
1 tablespoon sugar
3 cups fish stock
3 tablespoons chopped cilantro
½ cup all-purpose flour

*This Moroccan flavored snapper still manages to stay
light despite all of the flavors in it. I tend not to sear
the fish before serving but if you want some extra
flavor and texture you can sear it.*

Pre Bath
Preheat the water bath.

Salt and pepper each snapper filet and add
to the sous vide pouches. Split the olive oil
or butter equally among the pouches and
seal. Place into the water bath and cook for
10 to 30 minutes.

For the Sauce
Prepare the sauce about the same time you
put the fish in the sous vide bath.

Before cutting the fruits you can grate or
microplane the peel and add it later in the
cooking process or as a garnish for more
citrus flavor.

Peel the fruit and dice the flesh, removing all
the pith.

In a large pan over medium heat add the oil
and saute the onion and zucchini until it just
softens, about 2 to 3 minutes. Add the
saffron, diced pepper, and sugar and cook
for 1 minute. Add the fish stock and bring to
a boil.

Simmer for 10 minutes then add the citrus
and simmer for 10 more minutes. Take off
the heat and stir in the cilantro and ¾ of the
grated peels (if used). Set aside until ready
to plate.

Finishing
Take the fish out of the sous vide bath and
place on individual plates. Spoon the
saffron-citrus sauce over the top and serve.
It goes very well with roasted fingerling
potatoes or a plain risotto.

Mahi Mahi with Corn Salad

Time: 10 to 30 Minutes
Temperature: 122°F / 50°C for sushi quality or
132°F / 55.6°C otherwise
Serves: 4

For the Mahi Mahi
4 mahi mahi portions
1 teaspoons garlic powder
½ teaspoon onion powder
½ teaspoon paprika
¼ teaspoon cayenne pepper, or more to taste
Salt and pepper

For the Corn Salad
3 cups corn
½ pint cherry tomatoes, halved
1 red bell pepper, diced
2 tablespoons fresh basil, chopped

For the Dressing
2 tablespoons lime juice
1 teaspoon ancho chile powder
1 tablespoon olive oil
Salt and pepper

1 tablespoon fresh basil, chopped, for garnish
1 lime, quartered, for garnish

Mahi Mahi is a full flavored fish that can stand up to bolder ingredients. Here we pair it with some summer vegetables and a lime vinaigrette with some moderate heat. For a spicier dish you can add sliced serrano or jalapeno peppers to the dressing.

Pre Bath
Preheat the water bath to the indicated temperature.

Salt and pepper each mahi mahi filet and add to the sous vide pouches. Mix together the garlic powder, onion powder, paprika, and cayenne. Sprinkle the spice mixture on top of the fish and seal. Place into the water bath and cook for 10 to 30 minutes.

Finishing
Preheat the oven to 400°F.

Place the corn kernels and red pepper on a baking tray with raised edges. Drizzle olive oil over the top and salt and pepper. Cook until the kernels are soft, 5 to 10 minutes.

In a large bowl, combine the corn, tomatoes, roasted red pepper and basil and mix well. In a small bowl whisk together the ingredients for the dressing and pour over the corn.

Take the mahi mahi out of the pouch and pat dry. Sear over high-heat in a hot pan or on a hot grill, about 1 to 2 minutes per side.

To serve, take a large spoonful of the corn mixture and place on individual plates. Place the mahi-mahi on top. Top with a lime wedge and the basil and serve.

Lemon-Tarragon Swordfish

Time: 15 to 30 Minutes
Temperature: 132°F / 55.5°C
Serves: 2

For the Swordfish
2 swordfish portions
1 tablespoon butter
Salt and pepper

For the Butter
½ stick butter, softened at room temperature
2 tablespoons fresh tarragon, finely chopped
1 teaspoon grated lemon zest
⅛ teaspoon ground black pepper

The flavor of the swordfish is brightened by the lemon-tarragon butter and it is also a very quick and easy dish to make. This dish is great with steamed vegetables or a light risotto.

Pre-Bath
Preheat the water bath to 132°F / 55.5°C.

Salt and pepper the swordfish then add to the sous vide pouches. Add the butter and then seal and place in the water bath. Cook the swordfish for 15 to 30 minutes.

Finishing
To make the butter place all of the butter ingredients in a bowl and mix and mash thoroughly using a fork.

Take the swordfish out of the pouch and pat dry. Sear it on a very hot grill or in a hot pan, about 1 to 2 minutes per side. Place the swordfish on a plate and place a dollop or two of the butter on top.

Halibut with Tomato-Olive Vinaigrette

Time: 10 to 30 Minutes
Temperature: 129°F / 53.9°C for sushi quality or
132°F / 55.6°C otherwise
Serves: 4

For the Halibut
4 halibut portions
2 tablespoons butter or olive oil
Salt and pepper

For the Vinaigrette:
1 tablespoon red wine vinegar
1 tablespoon lemon juice
½ teaspoon garlic, minced
⅓ cup olive oil

½ cup cherry tomatoes, halved
3 tablespoons olives, preferably kalamata, pitted
and coarsely chopped
1 tablespoon fresh parsley, chopped
2 tablespoons pine nuts, toasted
Salt and pepper

*Adding a vinaigrette to a dish is an easy way to
introduce additional flavors without overpowering the
fish. Here we use a mild vinaigrette in addition to
tomatoes and olives to add flavor. This dish is great
when served over risotto, with creamy polenta, or
mashed potatoes.*

Pre Bath
Preheat the water bath to the indicated
temperature.

Salt and pepper each halibut portion and
add to the sous vide pouches. Add the
butter or olive oil and and seal. Place into
the water bath and cook for 10 to 30
minutes.

Finishing
In a small bowl combine the vinegar, lemon
juice, garlic and salt and pepper. Slowly
whisk in the olive oil.

Take the halibut out of the pouches and
place on a plate, preferably with risotto or
creamy polenta. Top with the tomato and
olives. Spoon the vinaigrette over the top,
sprinkle with the parsley and pine nuts and
serve.

Cod with Spicy Bean Salad

Time: 10 to 30 Minutes
Temperature: 129°F / 53.9°C for sushi quality or
132°F / 55.6°C otherwise
Serves: 4

For the Cod
4 cod portions
½ teaspoon ground cumin
2 tablespoons butter or olive oil
Salt and pepper

For the Salad
1 15-ounce can black beans, drained and washed
1 15-ounce can pinto beans, drained and washed
2 cups corn kernels
1 orange or red bell pepper, diced
1 poblano pepper, diced
1 shallot, diced
¼ cup red onion, finely diced
¼ cup fresh cilantro, chopped

For the Vinaigrette
½ teaspoon ground cumin
½ teaspoon ancho chile powder
⅛ teaspoon cayenne powder
6 tablespoons fresh lime juice
5 tablespoons olive oil
½ teaspoon salt
½ teaspoon black pepper

Often times cod is a blander fish. We try to spice it up here with a hearty bean salad with a spicy vinaigrette. We recommend ancho chile powder and poblano peppers but you can use any type of chile powder or hot pepper that you prefer.

Pre Bath

Preheat the water bath to the indicated temperature.

Salt and pepper each cod portion, sprinkle with the ground cumin, and add to the sous vide pouches. Add the butter or olive oil and and seal. Place into the water bath and cook for 10 to 30 minutes.

Finishing

Cook the corn, peppers, and onion in a 350°F oven for 5 to 10 minutes.

In a small bowl combine the spices, lime juice, and salt and pepper. Slowly whisk in the olive oil.

In a large bowl combine the beans, corn, peppers, onion, shallot, and cilantro. Add enough vinaigrette to thoroughly coat the salad.

Take the cod out of the pouches and pat dry. Sear one side over high heat on a grill or hot pan just until browned, one to two minutes. Remove from the heat.

To serve get 4 plates. On each plate put a spoonful of the salad with the cod, seared side up, resting on the top.

Scrod with Fennel Coleslaw

Time: 10 to 30 Minutes
Temperature: 122°F / 50°C for sushi quality or
132°F / 55.6°C otherwise
Serves: 4

For the Scrod
4 scrod portions
2 tablespoons butter or olive oil
Salt and pepper

For the Slaw
1 small fennel bulb, trimmed, cored, and
shredded
5 large carrots, peeled and shredded
1 cup snow pea pods, cut into long strips
¼ red onion, minced
½ cup fresh cilantro, chopped
⅓ cup sliced almonds, toasted

For the Vinaigrette
5 tablespoons orange juice, preferably fresh
1 tablespoon white wine vinegar
2 teaspoons yellow mustard
3 tablespoons olive oil
½ teaspoon salt
½ teaspoon pepper

*Coleslaw is often overlooked as a good side dish and
here we make a more upscale version with fennel,
carrots, and pea pods. It adds a great crunchy texture
to the silky, mild fish.*

Pre Bath
Preheat the water bath to the indicated
temperature.

Salt and pepper each scrod portion, sprinkle
with the ground cumin, and add to the sous
vide pouches. Add the butter or olive oil
and seal. Place into the water bath and cook
for 10 to 30 minutes.

Finishing
Whisk together all of the vinaigrette
ingredients in a bowl.

Combine the fennel, carrots, pea pods, red
onion and cilantro in a bowl.

Take the scrod out of the pouches and pat
dry. Sear one side over high heat on a grill or
hot pan just until browned, one to two
minutes. Remove from the heat.

To serve get 4 plates. Pour the dressing over
the slaw and mix well. On each plate put a
spoonful of the slaw with the scrod, seared
side up, resting on the top. Top with the
toasted almonds.

Hot and Smoky Mahi Mahi

Time: 10 to 30 Minutes
Temperature: 122°F / 50°C for sushi quality or
132°F / 55.6°C otherwise
Serves: 4

For the Mahi Mahi
4 portions of mahi mahi, 1 to 2 pounds
½ teaspoon cumin
1 teaspoon coriander
Salt and pepper

For the Butter
½ stick butter, softened at room temperature
¼ to 1 teaspoon chipotle puree
½ teaspoon paprika
⅛ teaspoon ground black pepper

*The flavor of the mahi mahi is deepened and enhanced
by this hot and smoky butter. You can add more or
less of the chipotle peppers to get to the hotness you
prefer. To make the chipotle puree simply process a can
of chipotle peppers in adobo sauce in a blender or food
processor until smooth. This dish is great with roasted
root vegetables.*

Pre-Bath
Preheat the water bath to the indicated
temperature.

Salt and pepper the mahi mahi then add to
the sous vide pouches. Add the butter and
then seal and place in the water bath. Cook
the mahi mahi for 10 to 30 minutes.

Finishing
To make the butter place all of the butter
ingredients in a bowl and mix and mash
thoroughly using a fork.

Take the mahi mahi out of the pouches and
pat dry. Sear it on a very hot grill or in a hot
pan, 1 to 2 minutes per side. Place the mahi
mahi on a plate and place a dollop or two of
the butter on top.

Sea Bass with Herb Salad

Time: 15 to 30 Minutes
Temperature: 122°F / 50°C for sushi quality,
otherwise 132°F / 55.5°C
Serves: 2

For the Sea Bass
2 portions of sea bass
2 tablespoons butter
Salt and pepper

For the Herb Salad
1 cup mixed soft herbs like basil, oregano,
parsley, tarragon, chives, mint and chervil
1 cup frisée lettuce, coarsely chopped
1 lemon
1 tablespoon olive oil
Salt and pepper

*The strong flavor of the herb salad helps to spruce up
the sea bass. This herb salad is great with many
different kinds of fish and can even be used with a
fattier cut of steak like a ribeye. This dish is great
when served with a side of roasted potatoes or a hearty
risotto.*

Pre-Bath
Preheat the water bath to the indicated
temperature.

Season the sea bass with the salt and pepper
then add to the sous vide pouch. Add the
butter to the pouch and then seal. Place in
the water bath and cook for 15 to 30
minutes.

Finishing
Take the sea bass out of the pouch, reserving
the butter liquid. If searing, pat dry the sea
bass and sear over high-heat in a hot pan or
on a hot grill.

Place the sea bass on the plates and top with
the herbs and frisée. Sprinkle with salt and
pepper. Spoon some of the juices from the
sous vide pouch over top of the greens.
Drizzle the olive oil over top and squeeze
the lemon equally over the two portions.

Blackened Grouper Caesar Salad

Time: 15 to 30 Minutes
Temperature: 122°F / 50°C for sushi quality,
otherwise 132°F / 55.5°C
Serves: 4

For the Grouper
1 pound of grouper, cut in 4 portions
1 tablespoon butter
½ teaspoon ground cumin
½ teaspoon garlic powder
½ teaspoon onion powder
½ teaspoon ground coriander
¼ teaspoon cayenne pepper, or to taste
Salt and pepper

1 head romaine lettuce, coarsely chopped
2 cups croutons
½ cup parmesan cheese, freshly grated

For the Dressing
1 egg yolk
2 anchovy filets
1 teaspoon Dijon mustard
1 teaspoon minced garlic
3 tablespoons fresh lemon juice
½ cup olive oil
Salt and pepper

*This recipe is a take off of a traditional caesar salad
and is very good with any white, mild fish. You can
also use chicken instead of fish. To make your own
fresh croutons you can see the Pesto Turkey Breast
Salad recipe. You can also use your favorite bottle of
caesar dressing to save time.*

Pre-Bath
Preheat the water bath to the indicated
temperature.

In a small bowl mix together the spices.
Season the grouper with the salt and pepper
then sprinkle with the spices. Add to the
sous vide pouch along with the butter and
seal.

Place the sous vide pouch into the water
bath and cook for 15 to 30 minutes.

Finishing
First, make the dressing. Place the egg yolks,
anchovies, garlic, mustard and lemon juice
into a food processor and process until
thoroughly mixed. With the food processor
still running slowly add the oil. Add salt
and pepper, tasting until the seasoning is
right.

Take the grouper out of the pouch and pat
dry. Sear the grouper over high-heat in a hot
pan until just browned, about 1 minute per
side.

Place the lettuce in a large bowl. Add
enough dressing to coat and toss the lettuce
to evenly mix. Place the coated lettuce on
individual plates. Top with the grouper,
parmesan cheese, and croutons. Crack some
fresh pepper on top and serve.

Haddock with Herby Vinaigrette

Time: 15 to 30 Minutes
Temperature: 122°F / 50°C for sushi quality,
otherwise 132°F / 55.5°C
Serves: 4

For the Haddock
1 ½ pounds of haddock, cut in 4 portions
1 tablespoon butter
Salt and pepper

For the Vinaigrette
2 tablespoons white wine vinegar
½ tablespoon shallot, minced
1 garlic clove, minced
Salt and pepper
6 tablespoons olive oil
¼ cup fresh basil, chopped
¼ cup fresh parsley, chopped

This recipe is very good with any white, mild fish. You can also play around with the herbs in the vinaigrette, mix and matching to your preference. Combined with steamed vegetables this dish makes a nice, light meal.

Pre-Bath
Preheat the water bath to the indicated temperature.

Season the haddock with the salt and pepper. Add to the sous vide pouch along with the butter and seal. Place the sous vide pouch into the water bath and cook for 15 to 30 minutes.

Finishing
First, make the vinaigrette. Combine the vinegar, shallot, garlic, and salt and pepper in a small bowl. Let sit for 5 minutes. Slowly whisk in the olive oil then stir in the herbs.

Take the haddock out of the sous vide pouches and pat dry. Sear it over high-heat in a hot pan until just browned, about 1 minute per side.

Serve the haddock with the vinaigrette spooned over it.

Shaved Fennel and Salmon

Time: 15 to 30 Minutes
Temperature: 122°F / 50°C for sushi quality,
otherwise 132°F / 55.5°C
Serves: 2

2 salmon filets, about a pound total, skin
removed
1 tablespoon butter
2 thyme sprigs
Salt and pepper
1 fennel bulb
1 lemon
1 ½ tablespoons olive oil

*The licorice flavor of the fennel pairs well with the
fatty flavors of the salmon. It is also great when
served with a side of roasted potatoes or a hearty
risotto. This fennel salad can be used on many types
of fish or even leaner meat like pork chops.*

Pre-Bath

Preheat the water bath to the indicated
temperature.

Season the salmon with the salt and pepper
then add to the sous vide pouch. Add the
butter and thyme to the pouch and then
seal.

Place the sous vide pouch into the water
bath and cook for 15 to 30 minutes.

Finishing

While the salmon is cooking prepare the
fennel. Remove any discolored outer layers,
the core, and the stalks, reserving some of
the fronds for garnish. Then thinly slice the
fennel. Using a mandolin is quicker and
easier than using a knife. The thinner you
cut it the more tender it will taste.

Take the salmon out of the pouch, pat dry
and sear quickly over high-heat in a hot pan
about 1 minute per side.

Place the salmon on plates and top with the
fennel slices. Sprinkle with salt and pepper.
Drizzle the olive oil over top and squeeze
the lemon equally over the two portions.
Add the fronds for garnish and serve.

Spicy Octopus

Time: 2 to 3 Hours
Temperature: 180°F / 82.2°C
Serves: 4 to 6

1 pound octopus, cleaned and cut into medium-sized pieces
1 tablespoon olive oil
3 garlic cloves, chopped
¼ teaspoon black pepper
2-4 small red chilies, finely chopped
1 tablespoon fish sauce
1 lime, sliced
1 tablespoon basil, chopped

This is a simple preparation for octopus and uses a marinade to help impart more flavor into it. This goes great with a nice salad of mixed greens, some wild rice, or even angel hair pasta with olive oil.

Pre-Bath
Preheat the water bath to 180°F / 82.2°C.

Combine the octopus, olive oil, garlic, pepper and chilies in a bowl and marinate for 30 minutes.

Remove the octopus from the marinade and place in a sous vide pouch. Seal the pouch and cook for 2 to 3 hours.

Finishing
Remove the octopus from the pouches and place on a plate. Sprinkle the fish sauce and basil on top and serve with a slice or two of lime on the side to squeeze over the dish.

Shrimp and Pumpkin Soup

Time: 15 to 35 Minutes
Temperature: 122°F / 50°C for sushi quality or
132°F / 55.6°C otherwise
Serves: 4 to 6

For the shrimp
8 large raw shrimp, peeled and deveined
1 tablespoon butter or olive oil
Salt and pepper

For the Soup
1 pound pumpkin
4 tablespoons lime juice
2 yellow or white onions, chopped
1 or 2 small red chilies, finely chopped
1 stem lemon grass (white part only), chopped
(optional)
1 teaspoon shrimp paste (optional)
1 teaspoon sugar
1 ½ cups coconut milk
1 teaspoon tamarind paste or puree (optional, if
omitted use 1 teaspoon worcester sauce)
1 cup water
½ cup coconut cream (optional, if omitted add ½
cup of coconut milk)
1 tablespoon fish sauce
2 tablespoons fresh Thai or italian basil, chopped

*While this recipe calls for many exotic ingredients
they can be left out and the soup will still be very
good. I've marked the ones that aren't critical to the
soup as optional but I would try to add in as many as
possible for the deepest flavor.*

Pre-Bath
Preheat the water bath to the indicated
temperature.

Add the shrimp to the sous vide pouches
and split the butter evenly among them.
Sprinkle with salt and pepper and seal.
Place in the water bath for 15 to 35 minutes.

For the Soup
Peel the pumpkin and remove the seeds
then cut the flesh into 1" chunks. For an
added garnish you can roast the seeds with
canola oil and salt in a 300°F oven for 10 to
20 minutes until they just start to brown and
then sprinkle them over the finished dish.

In a food processor combine the onions,
chili, lemon grass, shrimp paste, sugar and
about ½ of the coconut milk until well
mixed. In a large pot combine the onion
puree with the remaining coconut milk,
tamarind puree and water.

Add the pumpkin to the pot and bring to a
boil. Then reduce the heat, cover, and
simmer until the pumpkin begins to soften,
about 10 minutes.

Finishing
Take the shrimp out of the sous vide
pouches and add them to the soup. Stir in
the coconut cream, lime juice, and basil.
Ladle the soup into bowls and serve with
fresh, crusty bread.

Squid with Sugar-Snap Peas

Time: 2 to 4 Hours
Temperature: 138°F / 45°C
Serves: 4

For the Squid
14 ounces squid, cleaned
Salt and pepper

For the Peas
3 cups sugar-snap peas, cleaned
½ onion, cut into ¼" strips
1 orange or yellow bell pepper, cut into strips
1 red bell pepper, cut into strips
2 tablespoons sesame oil
4 garlic cloves, minced
2 teaspoons fresh ginger, grated
3 tablespoons soy sauce
6 tablespoons oyster sauce
5 tablespoons rice wine vinegar
½ cup chicken stock
2 tablespoons cornstarch
4 tablespoons cold water

This is a good way to highlight squid while moving away from the breaded and fried calamari style. The peas and vegetables add a sweetness and help complement the squid flavor while the sauce adds richness and body to the dish.

Pre-Bath
Preheat the water bath to 138°F / 45°C.

Rinse the squid under cold running water and cut into rings or thin strips. Season the squid with salt and pepper and seal in the sous vide pouch. Add to the water bath and cook for 2 to 4 hours, until it becomes tender.

Finishing
About 10 minutes before the squid is done start making the peas.

In a pan over medium heat add the oil and warm. Add the onion and cook until it turns translucent, about 5 minutes. Add the peas, peppers, ginger, and garlic and cook for 3 more minutes. Add the soy sauce, oyster sauce, vinegar, and stock and simmer for 2 minutes.

In a separate bowl whisk the cornstarch and cold water together. Add this to the pan with the peas and sauce while stirring quickly. Bring to a boil. Remove the squid from the sous vide pouches and pat dry and add to the pan. Stir well and remove from the heat.

Serve the squid in a deep plate or bowl with white or basmati rice.

Shrimp Bisque

Time: 15 to 35 Minutes
Temperature: 122°F / 50°C for sushi quality or
132°F / 55.6°C otherwise
Serves: 4 to 8

For the Shrimp
1½ pounds medium shrimp, still in the shell
½ teaspoon paprika powder
Salt and pepper

For the Bisque
3 tablespoons olive oil
3 tablespoons butter
2 leaks, rinsed and the bottom parts coarsely
chopped
1 onion, coarsely chopped
2 celery stalks, coarsely chopped
2 carrots, peeled and coarsely chopped
4 fresh thyme sprigs
1 bay leaf
3 tablespoons tomato paste
½ teaspoon chipotle pepper or cayenne powder
½ teaspoon sweet paprika
¼ cup brandy
¼ cup flour
3 cups heavy cream
1 cup whole milk
Salt and pepper
2 tablespoons fresh basil, chopped
1 tablespoon orange zest, preferably fresh

Cooking the shrimp for this bisque using sous vide
ensures that they will be perfectly cooked. You still get
the classic bisque flavor by sautéing the reserved
shells and making a quick seafood stock.

Pre-Bath
Peel and devein the shrimp and set aside the
shells for use in the stock. Sprinkle the
shrimp with the paprika and then salt and
pepper them. Place them in the sous vide
pouches and seal them.

The bisque takes longer to make than the
shrimp do to cook so you should set them
aside for now. After about 30 minutes into
making the bisque you will want to put the
shrimp into the water bath.

Finishing
You first want to make a simple seafood
stock from the shrimp shells.

Add the olive oil and butter to a large pot
set to medium high heat. Add the shrimp
shells, leeks, onion, celery, and carrots and
cook for about 5 minutes stirring every
minute or so. Add the thyme, bay, tomato
paste, paprika, and cayenne and stir well.
Cook for an additional 5 to 7 minutes until
the vegetables begin to soften, stirring
regularly.

Remove the pot from the heat and pour in
the brandy. Put the pot back on the stove
and reduce the heat to medium and cook
until the brandy begins to reduce, 1 or 2
minutes. Stir in the flour and cook for
another 2 to 3 minutes.

Add enough water to cover the ingredients,
about 3 cups. When adding the water scrape
the bottom of the pan with a wooden spoon
to deglaze it. Pour in the cream and bring it
to a boil. As soon as it boils turn the heat to
low and reduce it to a simmer for about 30
to 35 minutes until the bisque has reduced

and thickened. During this step you can put the shrimp into the sous vide bath.

Once the bisque and shrimp are done, pour the bisque through a strainer and into a clean pot. Season with salt and pepper, tasting as you season to keep it balanced. Ladle the soup into bowls, add some shrimp, and top with the orange zest and basil flakes. Serve with warm rolls or bread for soaking up the bisque.

Hot Buttered Lobster Rolls

Time: 15 to 35 Minutes
Temperature: 126°F / 52.2°C for sushi quality or
140°F / 60°C otherwise
Serves: 4

2 lobsters, 1 to ½ pounds each, parboiled and
meat removed then coarsely chopped
6 tablespoons butter
4 thyme sprigs
4 New-England style hot dog buns, split at the
top
1 teaspoon fresh tarragon, chopped
4 lemon wedges

*These rolls are very simple to make and are deliciously
rich. Just serve them with nice potato chips, coleslaw
or french fries and you're all set to close your eyes and
pretend you're at the beach.*

Pre-Bath

Preheat the water bath to 126°F / 52.2°C for
sushi quality or 140°F / 60°C otherwise.

Place the parboiled lobster meat, the butter,
and the thyme sprigs in the sous vide
pouches. Sprinkle with salt and pepper then
seal the pouches and place in the water bath
to cook for 15 to 35 minutes.

Finishing

Warm the buns in the oven. Remove the
lobster meat from the sous vide pouches and
place on the buns. Spoon some of the liquid
from the sous vide pouch on top of the rolls.
Top with the fresh tarragon and serve with
the lemon wedges.

Lobster Salad Rolls

Time: 15 to 35 Minutes
Temperature: 126°F / 52.2°C for sushi quality or
140°F / 60°C otherwise
Serves: 4

2 lobsters, 1 to ½ pounds each, parboiled and
meat removed then coarsely chopped
6 tablespoons butter
4 thyme sprigs
½ cup mayonnaise
1 celery stalk, diced
½ sweet red bell pepper, diced
1 tablespoon minced shallots
1 tablespoon fresh parsley, chopped
1 teaspoon chives, finely chopped
4 lemon wedges
4 New-England style hot dog buns, split at the
top

*This is the other classic lobster roll preparation. Like
the hot buttered rolls, just serve them with nice potato
chips, coleslaw or french fries for a great lunch.*

Pre-Bath
Preheat the water bath to 126°F / 52.2°C for
sushi quality or 140°F / 60°C otherwise.

Place the parboiled lobster meat, the butter,
and the thyme sprigs in the sous vide
pouches. Sprinkle with salt and pepper then
seal the pouches and place in the water bath
to cook for 15 to 35 minutes.

Finishing
Mix together the mayonnaise, celery, red
pepper, shallots, parsley, and chives in a
bowl.

Remove the lobster meat from the sous vide
pouches and place in the bowl with the
mayonnaise. Stir together and refrigerate for
10 to 15 minutes to chill the lobster and let
the flavors meld.

When ready to serve place the lobster
mixture on the buns and serve.

Fruits and Vegetables

Cooking vegetable and fruits sous vide is a great way to tenderize them without losing as much of the vitamins and minerals that are normally lost through blanching or steaming. Fruits can also be infused with liquid when cooked at lower temperatures when liquid is added to the bag.

Sous vide helps preserve the nutrients present in fruits and vegetables by not cooking them above the temperature that cause the cell walls to fully break down. This allows them to tenderize without losing all their structure. The bag also helps to catch any nutrients that do come out of the vegetable.

People do not love all vegetables cooked sous vide but some vegetables really can benefit with this cooking method. It's worth experimenting and seeing which ones you prefer.

Interested in sous vide shirts, aprons, and mugs?
We have a bunch of different gear you can buy in our online store.

You can find the sous vide gear at:
www.zazzle.com/cooking_sous_vide

Time and Temperature Guidelines

While time and temperature do not factor into safety for fruits and vegetables they do have a unique effect on their structure. There are two components to vegetables that make them crisp, pectin and starch. Pectin, which is basically a type of glue and is also used in jams and jellies for structure, breaks down at 183°F at a slower rate than the starch cells do. In many cases this allows for more tender vegetables that have a unique texture to them.

The time component just governs how long the starches and pectin are breaking down for and how tender the vegetable will become.

General Process

Cooking vegetables with sous vide is very simple and fast.

First, preheat your sous vide machine to the temperature desired, normally 183°F for most vegetables and many fruits.

Skin the vegetable if desired and place it in a sous vide pouch, sealing it with any normal seasoning such as:

- Fresh or dried thyme or rosemary
- Any spice powders such as onion, garlic, paprika, coriander, or cumin
- Chile powders like ancho, chipotle, cayenne
- Butter, olive oil, etc.

If adding a liquid, make sure your vacuum sealer does not suck it out, you can normally seal it before all the air is out to prevent this. Also, try to avoid fresh garlic or ginger as they can begin to take on a bad flavor over the longer cooking times.

After sealing the pouch place it into the water bath for the indicated cooking time. You might have to weigh the pouch down with a plate or lid.

Once it's fully cooked remove it from the pouch and pat dry. You can use it as you would normally by eating it plain, adding it to a rice or stir fry or any other use.

Moroccan Carrots

Time: 45 Minutes
Temperature: 183°F / 83.9°C
Serves: 4 as a side

4 large carrots, peeled and chopped into ½"
pieces
1 tablespoon butter or olive oil
1 teaspoon white vinegar
1 tablespoon honey
2 teaspoons sweet paprika
1 teaspoon chile powder
1 teaspoon salt
4 tablespoons fresh parsley, chopped

*These carrots add a lot of savoriness through the chile
powder and paprika.*

Pre-Bath
Preheat the water bath to 183°F / 83.9°C.

Combine all ingredients except the parsley
into a sous vide pouch and seal. Place in the
water bath and cook for 45 to 60 minutes.

Finishing
Once the carrots are tender remove from the
pouch and place directly on the plate. Top
with the parsley and sprinkle some coarse
salt over the top.

Fingerling Potato Salad

Time: 30 to 60 Minutes
Temperature: 183°F / 83.9°C
Serves: 4 as a side

3 pounds small fingerling potatoes, cleaned but skin on
½ teaspoon pepper
1 tablespoon fresh thyme
1 teaspoon salt
¼ pound bacon, cut crosswise into strips
2 carrots, diced
3 shallots, diced
2 garlic cloves, diced
1 celery stalk, diced
¼ cup mayonnaise
2 tablespoons apple cider vinegar
2 tablespoons Dijon mustard
2 tablespoons parsley, chopped
1 tablespoon tarragon, chopped

This is a unique mustard-vinegar potato salad which has a tartness not found in the typical mayonnaise based potato salads. The vinegar also helps this dish to complement fattier main courses like ribeye or duck breast.

Pre-Bath

Preheat the water bath to 183°F / 83.9°C.

Place the potatoes in a sous vide pouch and add the pepper, thyme, and salt. Seal the pouches and place in the water bath for 30 to 60 minutes, until the potatoes are tender.

Finishing

While the potatoes are cooking finish preparing the dish.

In a pan over medium heat saute the bacon until it begins to crisp and the fat is rendered. Remove ½ of the bacon fat from the pan. Add the carrots, garlic, and shallots to the pan and cook until the garlic and shallots become soft, about 5 minutes.

Remove the potatoes from the sous vide pouches and place into a large bowl. Pour the onion-garlic-bacon mixture over the top of the potatoes and stir to mix.

In a separate container mix together the mayonnaise, vinegar, and mustard. Pour it on top of the potatoes and mix well. Sprinkle the parsley and tarragon on top and serve.

Vanilla Poached Pears

Time: 60 to 90 Minutes
Temperature: 185°F / 85°C
Serves: 2

2 ripe medium pears, such as Bartlett, peeled,
halved through the stem end, and cored
1 lemon, halved
2 tablespoons unsalted butter, softened
1 ½ tablespoons sugar
1 teaspoon vanilla paste[22]
¼ teaspoon ground star anise
1 vanilla bean, halved lengthwise

*This recipe comes from Pam McKinstry from
SVKitchen.com, here's what she had to say about it:*

*Pears are one of my least loved fruits when eaten out
of hand, but when they're poached in butter, sugar,
vanilla, and spice, well, that's another story.
Normally, you immerse the pears in a flavorful liquid,
such as wine or sugar syrup, and cook them on the
stove top. Then, after they're poached, the cooking
liquid needs to be reduced to concentrate its flavors.*

*Poaching the pears sous vide, however, creates pears
that are perfectly soft without the need for several
cups of liquid. Instead, a sweetened compound butter
melts and moistens the pears. While they cook, the
pears release their luscious juices, and voilà — the
undiluted essence of pear and vanilla is captured in
the food bag. To serve, slice and fan the pear halves,
top with the buttery juices, and before you know it,
you've got a lovely dessert. — Pam McKinstry*

Pre-Bath
Preheat the water bath to 185°F / 85°C.

Drizzle lemon juice over all surfaces of the
pears to prevent discoloration.

Mash the butter with the sugar, vanilla
paste, and star anise until well blended.
Place half of the compound butter in a food
bag and add 2 pear halves and a vanilla
bean half. Vacuum seal. Repeat with the
remaining ingredients.

Cook the pears in the water bath for 1 hour,
or until the pears are just tender. Depending
on the variety and ripeness of your pears,
this could take an additional 15 to 30
minutes.

Finishing
Remove the pears from the bags and reserve
the juices. Using a small knife, make several
parallel cuts starting 1" below the top (stem
end) of the pear, slicing lengthwise to the
base. Press gently to fan the slices. Repeat
with the remaining pears. Drizzle with the
warm juices and serve immediately.

Chipotle Sweet Potato Salad

Time: 45 to 60 Minutes
Temperature: 183°F / 83.9°C
Serves: 6 as a side

For the Potatoes
4 sweet potatoes
4 tablespoons butter
½ teaspoon ground cumin
½ teaspoon ground coriander
½ teaspoon ground cloves
½ teaspoon ancho chile powder
½ teaspoon kosher salt

For the Salad
2 cups corn kernels, cooked
2 cups canned black beans, rinsed and drained
3 shallots, diced
½ cup cilantro, chopped

For the Vinaigrette
1 chipotle chile from a can of chipotles in adobo
1 garlic clove, finely minced
2 tablespoons ketchup
6 tablespoons lime juice
1 tablespoon honey
½ cup olive oil
Salt and pepper

The chipotle adds a nice burn to the usually super sweet potatoes and helps turn this into a savory salad.

Pre-Bath
Preheat the water bath to 183°F / 83.9°C.

Peel the sweet potatoes and cut into ¾" to 1" chunks. Add them to the sous vide pouches along with the butter and the spices and seal. Cook for 45 to 60 minutes until the potatoes are soft.

Finishing
When the potatoes get close to finishing put together the rest of the salad.

First, make the dressing. Put the chipotle, garlic and ketchup into a blender and process until smooth. Add the lime juice, honey, salt and pepper, and process again. Slowly add the olive oil while processing until it is incorporated.

Warm the beans and corn either in a 350°F oven for 5 to 10 minutes or in the microwave, if you prefer.

Remove the potatoes from the sous vide pouches and place into a large serving dish. Add the corn, black beans, shallots, and cilantro and mix well. Spoon the dressing over the salad, tossing and tasting as you go so you don't over dress it.

Creamy Green Bean Salad

Time: 30 to 45 Minutes
Temperature: 183°F / 83.9°C
Serves: 4 as a side

1 pound green beans, washed and trimmed
¾ cup sour cream
¼ cup heavy cream
1 lemon, juiced
¼ cup olive oil
¼ cup pitted kalamata olives
2 teaspoons dill, chopped
Fresh dill sprigs, for garnish
Salt and pepper

These beans can also be made ahead of time and served cold. They are a heavy side, as far as beans go, and should be served with something with bolder flavors so they don't overpower the main course.

Pre-Bath

Preheat the water bath to 183°F / 83.9°C.

Place the green beans in a sous vide pouch and salt and pepper them. Seal the pouch and place in the water bath for 30 to 45 minutes, until they are tender.

Finishing

Put the sour cream, heavy cream, lemon juice, olive oil and salt and pepper in a blender and process until smooth.

Remove the green beans from the water bath and place in a bowl. Add the olives and dill. Pour the blended mixture over the green beans and mix well. Garnish with the dill sprigs and serve.

Rustic Garlic Mashed Potatoes

Time: 30 to 60 Minutes
Temperature: 183°F / 83.9°C
Serves: 4 as a side

2 pounds potatoes, coarsely diced
½ teaspoon pepper
1 tablespoon fresh thyme
2 tablespoons butter
1 ½ teaspoons salt
6 garlic cloves, peeled
4 tablespoons butter
½ cup whole milk or heavy cream
3 tablespoons fresh basil, chopped
2 tablespoon parsley, chopped

These potatoes go great with roast beef or a roasted chicken. The roasted garlic adds a nice bite and also a sweetness from the roasting process. They are also nice with some freshly grated parmesan cheese on top.

Pre-Bath

Preheat the water bath to 183°F / 83.9°C.

Place the potatoes in a sous vide pouch and add the pepper, thyme, salt, and 2 tablespoons of the butter. Seal the pouches and place in the water bath for 30 to 60 minutes, until the potatoes are tender.

Finishing

When you put the potatoes in the water bath start to roast the garlic. Wrap the garlic cloves in tin foil with some olive oil and salt and place in a 400°F oven for around 30 minutes, until soft. Remove and set aside to cool slightly.

Remove the potatoes from the sous vide pouches and place into a large bowl. Add the roasted garlic, remaining butter, basil and parsley and mash with a potato masher or large fork. Do not over mash or the potatoes will take on a tacky texture. Salt and pepper to taste and serve.

"Always Perfect" Glazed Carrots

Time: 45 Minutes
Temperature: 183°F / 83.9°C
Serves: 4 as a side

4 large carrots, peeled and chopped into ¾"
pieces
1 tablespoon butter
¾ tablespoon sugar
½ teaspoon salt
1 tablespoon fresh parsley, chopped

*This recipe works great for many types of vegetables
including radishes, turnips, parsnips, or pearl onions.
You can also try different herb combinations like
rosemary and thyme for a more savory dish or
tarragon and mint for a sweeter combination.*

Pre-Bath
Preheat the water bath to 183°F / 83.9°C.

Combine all ingredients except the parsley
in a sous vide pouch and seal. Place in the
water bath and cook for 45 to 60 minutes.

Finishing
Once the carrots are tender remove from the
pouch and place in a pan over high heat and
cook for 2 minutes, stirring constantly. Once
glazed, place them directly on the plate. Top
with the parsley, sprinkle on some coarse
salt and grind some pepper on top.

Homestyle Sweet Potatoes

Time: 45 to 60 Minutes
Temperature: 183°F / 83.9°C
Serves: 6 as a side

4 large sweet potatoes
1 cup unsalted butter, cut into ¼" slices
⅛ teaspoon ground nutmeg
1 tablespoon bourbon
Kosher salt and freshly ground black pepper

This chunky sweet potato dish is great with duck or a fattier cut of steak like ribeye. It is also good when paired with a blander food such as chicken or turkey breast.

Pre-Bath

Preheat the water bath to 183°F / 83.9°C.

Peel the sweet potatoes and cut into 1" to 2" chunks. Add them to the sous vide pouches along with ¼ cup of the butter. Add the ground nutmeg into the pouch. Seal the pouch and cook for 45 to 60 minutes until the potatoes are very soft.

Finishing

Remove the sweet potatoes and butter from the sous vide pouch and add to a pan set over low heat. Add in about ¼ cup of the butter and the bourbon and mash the potatoes using a potato masher. Gradually stir in the remaining ½ cup of butter. Season with salt and pepper to taste and serve.

Garlic Confit

Time: 60 to 90 Minutes
Temperature: 185°F / 85°C
Makes: 2 Cups

2 cups peeled garlic cloves, about 8 to 10 bulbs
4 cups canola oil

*Here is another recipe from the gang at
SVKitchen.com, this one from Sally MacColl:*

*Where raw garlic is a strong and easily identifiable
flavor, garlic confit is subtle and delicate, with an
elusive yet irresistible flavor for which, in my opinion,
there is no substitute. Even compared to roasted
garlic, which I love whether it's enhancing a recipe or
simply slathered on a piece of toasted baguette, garlic
confit is light and understated. It can add just the
right touch to a range of dishes, from poultry and
shellfish to soups and salad dressings, without
overpowering delicate ingredients.*

*Garlic confit is a staple in my kitchen. I always have
some on hand for that special flavor tweak. Preparing
it sous vide is a snap, so I do a pretty large
quantity, but you can easily cut this recipe in half. —
Sally MacColl*

Pre-Bath

Preheat the water bath to 185°F / 85°C.

Divide the peeled cloves equally into two
large, heavy-duty, double-zipper bags. Add
2 cups of canola oil to each of the bags and
seal them.

Cook the garlic cloves for 90 minutes, or
until they are very soft but still hold their
shape. You can test doneness by carefully
removing a bag from the water bath and
lightly pressing the back of a spoon or fork
against one of the cloves to make sure that it
is completely tender.

Finishing

Remove the bags from the water bath, open
them immediately, and transfer the garlic
and oil to lidded jars. Make sure the garlic is
completely covered by the oil, adding a little
fresh oil if necessary. Allow the garlic to cool
to room temperature before refrigerating for
up to a month.

Roasted Broccoli with Crispy Parmesan and Lemon

Time: 20 to 25 Minutes
Temperature: 183°F / 83.9°C
Serves: 4 as a side

1 head of broccoli
½ cup freshly grated Parmigiano-Reggiano cheese
1 lemon
Salt and pepper

This dish uses sous vide to perfectly cook the broccoli and then uses the broiler to melt the parmesan cheese to add a crispy texture and deeper flavor.

Pre-Bath
Preheat the water bath to 183°F / 83.9°C.

Cut the broccoli into large pieces and place into the sous vide pouch. Salt and pepper the broccoli and then seal the pouch. Place the pouch in the water bath and cook for 20 to 25 minutes.

Finishing
Preheat the broiler on the oven.

Remove the broccoli from the sous vide pouch and place in a roasting pan. Sprinkle the parmesan cheese over the top and place in the oven until the cheese melts and begins to crisp up. Take the broccoli out of the oven and place in the serving bowl. Squeeze the lemon over the top and serve.

Cauliflower with Spicy Chickpeas

Time: 20 to 30 Minutes
Temperature: 183°F / 83.9°C
Serves: 4 as a side

1 head of cauliflower
2 tablespoons butter or olive oil
Salt and pepper

For the Chickpeas
2 cups cherry tomatoes, halved
¼ red onion, thinly sliced
1 cup canned chickpeas, rinsed and drained
½ cup fresh cilantro, chopped

For the Vinaigrette
3 tablespoons lemon juice
1 serrano pepper, seeded and diced
¼ cup olive oil
Salt and pepper

Cauliflower is considered bland by many people so in this dish we use some spicy chickpeas to add some bold flavors. You can use any canned beans you have and each kind will add it's own flavor to the dish.

Pre-Bath
Preheat the water bath to 183°F / 83.9°C.

Cut the cauliflower into large pieces and place into the sous vide pouch with the butter. Salt and pepper the cauliflower and then seal the pouch. Place the pouch into the water bath and cook for 20 to 30 minutes, until soft.

Finishing
First make the vinaigrette. Combine the lemon juice, serrano pepper, and salt and pepper in a bowl, let sit for 3 to 5 minutes then slowly whisk in the olive oil.

Remove the cauliflower from the sous vide pouch and put in a large serving bowl. Add the chickpeas, tomatoes, red onion, and cilantro. Mix well then toss with enough of the dressing to coat but not overpower it.

Asparagus and White Bean Salad

Time: 30 to 40 Minutes
Temperature: 183°F / 83.9°C
Serves: 4 as a side

For the Asparagus
½ pound asparagus
1 tablespoon butter or olive oil
Salt and pepper

For the Salad
1 14-ounce can white beans
1 or 2 roasted red bell peppers, diced

For the Vinaigrette:
2 tablespoons red wine or apple cider vinegar
1 tablespoon shallot, minced
6 tablespoons olive oil
6 tablespoons fresh basil, minced
Salt and pepper

This side salad goes really well with mahi mahi or seared tuna. It is also good with turkey or chicken.

Pre-Bath
Preheat the water bath to 183°F / 83.9°C.

Cut the bottoms off of the asparagus and then cut into 1" pieces. Place into the sous vide pouch, add the butter and salt and pepper then seal the pouch. Place the pouch into the water bath and cook for 30 to 40 minutes.

Finishing
Combine the vinegar, shallot, and salt and pepper in a bowl, let sit for 3 to 5 minutes then slowly whisk in the olive oil and stir in the basil.

Take the asparagus out of the water bath and place into a serving bowl. Add the beans and peppers and toss. Add enough vinaigrette to coat the salad and add salt and pepper as needed.

Green Bean and Radicchio Salad

Time: 30 to 45 Minutes
Temperature: 183°F / 83.9°C
Serves: 4 as a side

1 pound fresh green beans, ends trimmed
1 tablespoon butter or olive oil
1 radicchio, thinly sliced
⅓ cup pecans
4 ounces feta cheese

For the Vinaigrette
1 tablespoon lemon juice
1 small garlic clove, minced
1 shallot, diced
3 tablespoons olive oil
Salt and pepper

The radicchio adds a nice bitterness to this light salad.

Pre-Bath
Preheat the water bath to 183°F / 83.9°C.

Place the green beans in a sous vide pouch with the butter then salt and pepper them. Seal the pouch and place in the water bath for 30 to 45 minutes, until they are tender.

Finishing
Soak the radicchio slices in cold water for 10 to 15 minutes, this will help to remove some of the bitterness.

Mix together the lemon juice, garlic, shallot and salt and pepper in a small bowl. Let sit for several minutes. Slowly whisk in the olive oil.

Remove the green beans from the water bath and place in a bowl. Add the radicchio. Coat with the vinaigrette and toss. Place a spoonful on a plate, top with the pecans and cheese, and serve.

"Braised" Leek Salad

Time: 30 to 60 Minutes
Temperature: 183°F / 83.9°C
Serves: 6 as a side or starter

For the Leeks
9 leeks
2 tablespoons fresh thyme
1 tablespoon lemon zest
2 bay leaves
¼ cup dry white wine
Salt and pepper

For the Dressing
½ cup olive oil
1 leek, white part only, thinly sliced
½ teaspoon Dijon or country mustard
2 tablespoons apple cider vinegar
1 tablespoon fresh tarragon, chopped
Salt and pepper

This leek salad is great as a starting or side course for a poached fish or roasted chicken. Cooking the leeks in the sous vide bath renders them very tender and mild.

Pre-Bath

Preheat the water bath to 183°F / 83.9°C.

Wash and trim the leeks by cutting off the top green portion and the bottom strings. Cut the root ends in half and add to a sous vide pouch. Add the thyme, lemon zest, bay leaves and white wine to the pouch and seal. Place in the water bath and cook for 30 to 60 minutes.

Finishing

Take the leeks out of the water bath and place in an ice water bath or in the refrigerator. While the leeks are cooling make the dressing.

Heat 1 tablespoon of the oil in a pan over medium heat. Add the sliced leek and cook until it turns soft, 10 to 15 minutes. Take off the heat and scrape into a bowl.

To the bowl with the sauteed leeks add the mustard, vinegar, salt and pepper and mix together. Slowly whisk in the olive oil.

Take the sous vide leeks out of the pouch and arrange on the plates. Spoon the dressing on top and sprinkle with salt and pepper and the tarragon.

Lamb

Some of the most impressive results of sous vide are created with tough cuts of lamb. Sous vide allows you to do things that traditional methods are unable to accomplish, such as cooking the roasts medium-rare and falling apart tender.

This is accomplished because cooking tough cuts of lamb with sous vide allows you to break down and tenderize the meat without cooking it above medium-rare and drying it out. Once temperatures in lamb go much above 140°F the meat begins to dry out and become more bland, however, they also start to tenderize more quickly which is why tough roasts and braises are done for hours at high temperatures. Using sous vide, you can hold the meat below 140°F for a long enough time for the tenderizing process to run its course.

I often use lamb cooked sous vide as a basis for many normal lamb dishes, such as leg of lamb, lamb stew, or lamb curry. You can also use it in any of your favorite recipes, simply replace the cooking step in the recipe with the already cooked sous vide lamb and then continue the rest of the recipe. Of course, it is also great eaten plain or with a simple sauce.

Time and Temperature Guidelines

The FDA states that lamb is safe when it is held at 130°F for over 112 minutes, or 140°F for over 12 minutes. This is very easy to do with sous vide and the main reason we recommend cooking most lamb cuts medium-rare since lamb is most tender at that temperature.

Additionally, the center of "whole" muscles are sterile but due to some mechanical tenderization that some meat packagers use the muscles can be compromised so unless you trust your supplier it is advisable to cook lamb to at least 130°F throughout.

Medium-rare lamb is cooked between 130°F to 139°F, we recommend cooking it at 131°F to give yourself a few degrees of temperature variation above the bottom of the safe zone but feel free to experiment with any temperatures in that range. Depending on the toughness of the cut of lamb, it may need to be cooked anywhere from 2 hours up to 2 or 3 days.

For each lamb cut we also give directions for medium. These are normally cooked between 140°F and 149°F, though we recommend not going above 140°F because the lamb begins drying out quickly and with sous vide there is no gain in food safety above 131°F.

Also, some lamb cuts benefit from higher temperatures to help further tenderize them. These dishes will result in a more traditional look and feel from the cut of meat and we have provided these for several of the cuts. These "Well / Traditional" entries will be "fork tender" like a normal braise would be.

We also provide time and temperatures for Rare lamb, but this results in an unpasteurized piece of meat so no bacteria will be killed in the cooking process and it could be harmful to your health unless the meat is completely heathy.

Most tough cuts of lamb are cooked sous vide for between 1 and 2 days. However, for some more tender lamb roasts shorter cooking times of 2 to 4 hours will be enough time to tenderize the meat fully.

General Process

The normal method of cooking tough cuts of lamb with sous vide is very simple. If the meat is over 3" wide then slice it into 2" slabs. If you want the roast to stay whole it is possible but you will need to add some cooking time to it.

Preheat your sous vide machine to the temperature desired, we recommend 131°F to 140°F for most cuts unless you are trying the "Well / Traditional" entry.

Take the meat and sprinkle it with salt and pepper and seal it into a sous vide pouch. You can also season the meat before sealing it with any normal seasoning such as:

- Fresh or dried thyme or rosemary
- Any spice powders such as onion, garlic, or paprika
- Chile powders like ancho, chipotle, cayenne
- Marinades
- Sauces like A1 steak sauce, worcester sauce, BBQ sauce, etc.

If adding a sauce or marinade make sure your vacuum sealer does not suck it out, you can normally seal it before all the air is out to prevent this. Also, we do not recommend using fresh garlic, onions, or ginger, as they can begin to take on a bad flavor over the long cooking times.

After sealing the pouch place it into the water bath for the indicated cooking time.

Once it's fully cooked remove it from the pouch and pat dry. At this point you can sear the meat in a hot skillet to add a nice crust to it or you can slice it and serve as is. You can also apply a normal roasted crust such as a garlic paste or horseradish and place it in a very hot oven until the crust sets, about 5 to 10 minutes.

Once the meat is done cooking you can use it as you would any typical lamb roast or braise. You can also make a nice gravy or pan sauce from the liquid leftover in the sous vide pouch.

Rosemary Mustard Lamb Chops

Time: 2 to 4 Hours
Temperature: 131°F / 55°C
Serves: 4

8-10 lamb chops

For the Rub
1 tablespoon whole yellow mustard seeds
¼ cup garlic, minced
6-8 rosemary sprigs, chopped
2 tablespoons Worcester sauce
2 tablespoons olive oil
2 tablespoons coarse salt (kosher or sea)
1 tablespoon dark brown sugar
2 teaspoons mustard powder
1 tablespoon cracked black pepper

This dish features a bold rosemary-mustard rub for the lamb chops that helps to bring out the natural flavors of the lamb.

For the Rub

Grind the mustard seeds in a spice grinder or place them in a ziploc bag and crack them by rolling over them with a rolling pin. Place the mustard seeds and remaining ingredients into a bowl and mix together.

Pre-Bath

Preheat the water bath to 131°F / 55°C.

Rub the rosemary-mustard paste all over the lamb chops. Place the lamb chops in the sous vide pouches and seal. Any excess paste can be refrigerated for about a week. Place the sous vide pouches into the water and cook for 2 to 4 hours.

Finishing

Take the lamb chops out of the sous vide bath and pat dry. On a very hot grill or pan set over medium-high heat sear the lamb chops, 1 to 2 minutes per side. Remove from the heat and serve.

Lamb Chops with Melon Relish

Time: 2 to 4 Hours
Temperature: 131°F / 55°C
Serves: 4

For the Lamb
8 lamb chops
1 teaspoon dried thyme
1 teaspoon garlic powder
Salt and pepper

For the Relish
¼ cup lime juice
2 tablespoons brown sugar
1 tablespoon fresh ginger, minced
½ teaspoon ground cinnamon
2 cups watermelon, diced
2 cups cantaloup or honeydew, diced
1 cucumber, peeled, seeded, and diced
½ cup red onion, diced
1 to 3 jalapeno chilies, seeded and diced
⅓ cup fresh mint, chopped

The relish in this dish features chunks of melon and cucumber which help to bring out the sweetness in the lamb and has a little heat from the jalapeno peppers for added bite.

Pre-Bath
Preheat the water bath to 131°F / 55°C.

Mix together the dried thyme, garlic powder, salt and pepper and sprinkle over the lamb chops. Place the lamb chops in the sous vide pouches and seal. Place the sous vide pouches into the water bath and cook for 2 to 4 hours.

Finishing
Up to 30 minutes before the lamb is done make the relish. Whisk the lime juice, brown sugar, ginger, and cinnamon in a bowl until the sugar is dissolved. Add the remaining ingredients and mix well.

Take the lamb chops out of the sous vide bath and pat dry. On a very hot grill or pan set over medium-high heat sear the lamb chops, 1 to 2 minutes per side.

Serve the lamb chops with a spoonful or two of the relish on top.

Spicy-Garlic Leg of Lamb

Time: 2 to 3 Days
Temperature: 131°F / 55°C
Serves: 4

1 pound lamb leg

For the Marinade
½ cup olive oil
¼ cup fresh parsley, coarsely chopped
¼ cup lemon juice
¼ cup fresh basil, coarsely chopped
4 garlic cloves, coarsely chopped
1 teaspoon hot pepper flakes
½ teaspoon black pepper
½ teaspoon salt

This leg of lamb has a nice garlic bite to it along with the heat from the pepper flakes. It is good when featured alongside a hearty risotto or mashed potatoes. You can also take the juice from the sous vide pouch and make a gravy with it, adding some veal or chicken stock if needed.

For the Marinade

Whisk together the lemon juice, pepper, hot pepper flakes, and salt in a bowl until the salt is dissolved. Add the garlic, parsley, and basil and whisk in the olive oil. Cover the lamb leg with the marinade and refrigerate for 8 to 12 hours.

Pre-Bath

Preheat the water bath to 131°F / 55°C.

Remove the lamb from the marinade and place it in a sous vide pouch. Sprinkle with salt and pepper and seal the pouch. Place the pouch in the water bath and cook for 2 to 3 days.

Finishing

Remove the lamb from the water bath and sous vide pouch. Pat it dry and sear over high heat on a grill or in a pan just until browned, 1 to 2 minutes per side. Slice the lamb into portions and serve.

Rustic Rack of Lamb

Time: 2 to 3 Hours
Temperature: 131°F / 55°C
Serves: 4

2 1-pound racks of lamb, frenched
4 rosemary sprigs
½ bunch fresh thyme
2 tablespoons butter or olive oil
1 cup veal or chicken stock
2 tablespoons cold water
2 tablespoons flour

This rack of lamb is very rustic and simple. It's great when served with homestyle mashed potatoes and roasted vegetables.

Pre-Bath
Preheat the water bath to 131°F / 55°C.

Place the lamb in a sous vide pouch with the rosemary, thyme, and butter. Sprinkle with salt and pepper and seal the pouch. Place the pouch in the water bath and cook for 2 to 3 hours.

Finishing
Remove the lamb from the water bath and sous vide pouches, reserving the liquid from the pouches. Pat the lamb dry.

Pour the reserved juices from the pouch into a cold pan on the stove and add the veal stock. In a small bowl whisk together the cold water and the flour then whisk into the pan. Turn the heat up and bring it to a simmer, stirring regularly, until it thickens.

Sear the lamb over high heat on a grill or in a pan until just browned, 1 to 2 minutes per side. Remove from the heat and cut the lamb into serving portions.

Serve the lamb with the gravy spooned on top or in a small dish on the side.

Leg of Lamb Salad with Creamy Mint Dressing

Time: 2 to 3 Days
Temperature: 131°F / 55°C
Serves: 4

For the Lamb
1 pound lamb leg
½ tablespoon fresh thyme
1 tablespoon fresh rosemary
Salt and pepper

For the Dressing
1 cup unflavored yogurt
½ cup mint leaves
½ cup golden raisins
1 ½ tablespoons lemon juice
¼ teaspoon pepper
Salt and pepper

For the Salad
Mixed greens
1 tomato, diced
¼ cup walnuts
¼ crumbled blue cheese

This salad is a full meal, especially if served with warm rolls or a baguette. The dressing contains the classic lamb pairings of yogurt and mint.

Pre-Bath
Preheat the water bath to 131°F / 55°C.

Season the lamb with salt and pepper and place into a sous vide pouch. Add the thyme and rosemary and seal. Place into the water bath and cook for 2 to 3 days.

Finishing
Right before you take the lamb out of the sous vide make the dressing. Put the yogurt, mint, and raisins into a blender and process until smooth. Add the lemon juice, salt, and pepper, and process briefly to combine.

Take the lamb out of the sous vide pouches and pat dry. Sear the lamb on a very hot grill or in a hot pan just until browned, about 1 to 2 minutes per side. Remove the lamb from the heat and slice it into strips.

On individual plates, top the mixed greens with the lamb slices and tomato. Drizzle the mint-raisin dressing over it. Sprinkle the walnuts and blue cheese on top and serve.

Apricot Lamb Tajine

Time: 2 to 4 Hours
Temperature: 131°F / 55°C
Serves: 2

For the Lamb
4 to 6 lamb chops
½ tablespoon sweet paprika
½ teaspoon saffron threads
¾ tablespoon chopped ginger
1 bay leaf
Salt and pepper

For the Sauce
2 white onions, sliced
1 tablespoon sweet paprika
½ teaspoon saffron threads
¾ tablespoon chopped ginger
1 bay leaf
Salt and freshly ground black pepper to taste
¼ cup olive oil
2 cups water
Juice of 2 oranges
½ cup honey
1 tablespoon ground cinnamon

8 dried apricots, cut into 1" pieces
½ cup roasted almonds

This is an exotic dish that really brings out the flavor of the lamb. It's best when served with rice or crusty bread to soak up all the sauce.

Pre-Bath
Preheat the water oven to 131°F / 55°C.

Combine the spices in a bowl and then rub on the lamb chops. Sprinkle with salt and pepper and seal in sous vide pouches. Place into the water bath and cook for 2 to 4 hours until the meat is tender.

For the Sauce
30 minutes before the lamb is done begin to make the sauce. In a pan over medium heat add the onions and cook until they begin to caramelize, about 10 minutes. Add the ginger and cook for 2 minutes. Add the paprika, saffron, bay leaf, orange juice, honey, water, and cinnamon and simmer for 15 minutes.

For added flavor you can stir in some of the juices from the sous vide pouch when you take the lamb out for browning.

Finishing
Once the lamb chops are done take them out of the sous vide pouch and pat dry. On a very hot pan or grill quickly brown each side of the lamb chop, about 1 minute per side. Remove and set aside.

Place the lamb chops on a deep plate or in a shallow bowl and pour the sauce over top. Top with the apricots and almonds and serve with a warm, crusty loaf of bread.

Mint-Fennel Lamb Shank

Time: 1 to 2 Days
Temperature: 131°F / 55°C
Serves: 4 to 6

For the Lamb
2 pounds lamb shank
2 thyme sprigs
2 rosemary sprigs
Salt and pepper

For the Butter
½ stick butter, softened at room temperature
1 tablespoon fresh mint, finely chopped
½ teaspoon fennel seeds
¼ teaspoon lemon zest, grated
⅛ teaspoon ground black pepper

The flavor of the lamb is brightened by the mint and fennel in the butter. A side of braised or roasted fennel complements this dish perfectly, as does mashed potatoes.

Pre-Bath
Preheat the water bath to 131°F / 55°C.

Salt and pepper the lamb shank then add to the sous vide pouches with the thyme and rosemary. Seal the pouch and place in the water bath to cook for 1 to 2 days.

Finishing
To make the butter place all of the butter ingredients in a bowl and mix and mash thoroughly using a fork.

Take the lamb shank out of the sous vide bath and pat dry. On a very hot grill or pan set over medium-high heat sear the lamb shank, 1 to 2 minutes per side.

Cut the lamb shank into portions, place on a plate and put a dollop or two of the butter on top.

Lamb Chops with Harissa

Time: 2 to 4 Hours
Temperature: 131°F / 55°C
Serves: 4 to 6

For the Lamb
12 lamb chops
1 teaspoon ground cumin
1 teaspoon ground coriander
Salt and pepper

For the Harissa
1 teaspoon ground cumin
1 teaspoon caraway seeds
1 large roasted red bell pepper, coarsely chopped
2 garlic cloves, coarsely chopped
2 small hot red chiles, coarsely chopped
1 teaspoon kosher salt
3 tablespoons olive oil
¼ cup cilantro, chopped
Juice of 1 lemon
4 tablespoons olive oil
Salt and pepper

Harissa is a hot chile sauce often eaten in North Africa. Here we use it to add bold flavors to the lamb chops.

Pre-Bath
Preheat the water bath to 131°F / 55°C.

Sprinkle the lamb chops with the cumin and coriander then salt and pepper them. Add to the sous vide pouches and seal. Place the pouches in the water bath and cook for 2 to 4 hours.

For the Harissa
Put all ingredients into a blender or food processor and process until pureed well. This can be stored in the refrigerator for several weeks.

Finishing
Take the lamb chops out of the sous vide bath and pat dry. On a very hot grill or pan set over medium-high heat sear the lamb chops, 1 to 2 minutes per side.

Serve the lamb chops with the harissa sauce spooned on top or in small bowls on the side.

Turkish Loin Roast

Time: 2 to 4 Hours
Temperature: 131°F / 55°C
Serves: 4 to 6

2 to 3 pounds lamb loin

For the Marinade
2 cups plain whole milk yogurt
½ cup olive oil
3 tablespoons lemon juice
1 onion, chopped
3 garlic cloves, minced
1 teaspoon salt
½ teaspoon black pepper
½ teaspoon hot pepper flakes

This marinade helps add a lot of flavor to the lamb loin. The yogurt also helps to slightly change the meat, making it more tender. The lamb is very good when served with some creamy polenta or rustic mashed potatoes.

For the Marinade
Place the yogurt in a bowl and mix in the rest of the marinade ingredients.

Cover the lamb loin with the marinade and refrigerate for 6 to 12 hours.

Pre-Bath
Preheat the water bath to 131°F / 55°C for medium-rare.

Remove the lamb from the marinade and place it in the sous vide pouch and seal. Place the pouch in the water bath and cook for 2 to 4 hours.

Finishing
Take the lamb loin out of the sous vide bath and pat dry. On a very hot grill or pan set over medium-high heat sear the lamb, 1 to 2 minutes per side. Remove from the heat and serve.

Tarragon-Lemon Lamb Chops

Time: 2 to 4 Hours
Temperature: 131°F / 55°C
Serves: 4 to 6

For the Lamb
12 lamb chops
1 teaspoon ground cumin
1 teaspoon garlic powder
Salt and pepper

For the Butter
½ stick butter, softened at room temperature
2 tablespoons fresh tarragon, finely chopped
1 garlic clove, finely minced
¼ teaspoon lemon zest, grated
⅛ teaspoon ground black pepper

The flavor of the lamb is brightened by this citrusy butter. The butter is quick to put together and very simple. This dish is great with steamed vegetables and rice.

Pre-Bath
Preheat the water bath to 131°F / 55°C.

Salt and pepper the lamb chops then sprinkle with the cumin and garlic powder. Add to the sous vide pouches and then seal. Place in the water bath and cook for 2 to 4 hours.

Finishing
To make the butter place all of the butter ingredients in a bowl and mix and mash thoroughly using a fork.

Take the lamb chops out of the sous vide bath and pat dry. On a very hot grill or pan set over medium-high heat sear the lamb chops, 1 to 2 minutes per side.

Place the lamb chops on a plate and place a spoonful or two of the butter on top.

Brazilian Lamb Chops

Time: 2 to 4 Hours
Temperature: 131°F / 55°C
Serves: 4 to 6

12 lamb chops

For the Marinade
6 garlic cloves, coarsely chopped
2 teaspoons salt
¼ cup lime juice
¼ cup white wine
1 tablespoon red wine vinegar
2 teaspoons hot sauce
3 tablespoons fresh parsley, coarsely chopped
1 tablespoon fresh rosemary, coarsely chopped
1 tablespoon fresh mint, coarsely chopped

Using this marinade before cooking the lamb chops deeply flavors the meat and adds moisture to the inside of the lamb. The lamb is great when served with a bold risotto or a salad of mixed greens.

For the Marinade
Place all of the marinade ingredients into a blender and pulse several times until mixed well. Cover the lamb chops with the marinade and refrigerate for 2 to 4 hours.

Pre-Bath
Preheat the water bath to 131°F / 55°C.

Remove the lamb chops from the marinade and place them in the sous vide pouches and seal. Place the pouches in the water bath and cook for 2 to 4 hours.

Finishing
Take the lamb chops out of the sous vide bath and pat dry. On a very hot grill or pan set over medium-high heat sear the lamb chops, 1 to 2 minutes per side. Remove from the heat and serve.

Lamb Curry

Time: 2 to 3 Days
Temperature: 131°F / 55°C
Serves: 4

For the Lamb
2 pounds boneless leg of lamb
1 teaspoon garam masala
Salt and pepper

For the Curry
3 onions, chopped
2 carrots, peeled and chopped
1 red bell pepper, chopped
3 tablespoons canola oil
5 garlic cloves
2-inch piece fresh ginger, peeled and cut into large chunks
2 teaspoons ground coriander
½ teaspoon black pepper
½ teaspoon ground cloves
¼ to 1 teaspoon cayenne pepper
½ teaspoon garam masala
½ cup plain yogurt, preferable whole milk
1 ½ cups water
¼ cup heavy cream
¼ cup fresh parsley, chopped
Salt and pepper

This is a classic curry featuring the lamb. It can also be used with chicken or pork. Serve with rice and bread to soak up sauce and maybe a crisp salad to offset the richness of the curry.

Pre-Bath
Preheat the water bath to 131°F / 55°C.

Cut the lamb into 1" to 2" chunks and season with the garam masala and salt and pepper. Place into the sous vide pouches and seal. Put the pouches into the water bath and cook for 2 to 3 days.

Finishing
About 30 to 45 minutes before the lamb is done start working on the curry.

Add ½ of the onion and all of the garlic and ginger to a food processor and process to a paste.

Warm a pan over medium-high heat with the canola oil in it. Add the remaining onion and cook until it begins to soften, about 5 minutes. Add the carrots and cook for another 5 minutes. Add the red bell pepper and cook for another 5 minutes.

Add the pureed onion mixture, the coriander, pepper, cayenne, garam masala, and cloves to the pan. Cook for about 10 minutes while stirring occasionally.

Add the yogurt and water and bring to a simmer. Remove the lamb from the sous vide pouches and add to the pan, along with some of the juices from the pouch. Stir well and let simmer for about 5 minutes.

Stir in the cream and parsley and serve, preferably over rice or with crusty bread.

Pork

There are two main benefits to cooking pork with sous vide. The first is that sous vide allows you to safely cook pork to medium-rare doneness. The other benefit is the ability to tenderize tougher cuts of pork through longer cooking times without drying them out.

This is accomplished because cooking pork with sous vide allows you to break down and tenderize the meat without cooking it above medium-rare and drying it out. Once temperatures in pork go above 140°F the meat begins to dry out and become more bland, however, they also start to tenderize more quickly which is why tougher cuts of pork are traditionally done for hours at high temperatures. Using sous vide, you can hold the meat below 140°F for a long enough time for the tenderizing process to run its course.

You can stay up to date with the current happenings in sous vide by reading our blog. We try to update it regularly with current information about sous vide.

You can find it at:
www.cookingsousvide.com/info/sous-vide-blog

Time and Temperature Guidelines

The FDA states that pork is safe when it is held at 130°F for over 112 minutes, or 140°F for over 12 minutes. This is very easy to do with sous vide and the main reason we recommend cooking most pork cuts medium-rare since it is most tender at that temperature. However, some people find the texture of truly medium-rare pork off-putting so a temperature of 138°F to 140°F might be more appealing.

Medium-rare pork is cooked between 130°F to 139°F, we recommend cooking it at 131°F to give yourself a few degrees of temperature variation above the bottom of the safe zone but feel free to experiment with any temperatures in that range. Depending on the toughness of the cut, it may need to be cooked anywhere from 2 hours for a pork chop up to 2 or 3 days for a picnic roast.

For each cut we also give directions for medium, these are normally cooked between 140°F and 149°F, though we recommend not going above 140°F because the meat begins drying out quickly and with sous vide there is no gain in food safety above 131°F and the color and texture is about the same at 140°F as it is at higher temperatures.

General Process

Cooking pork with sous vide is very simple.

First, preheat your sous vide machine to the temperature desired, we recommend 131°F to 140°F for most cuts.

If you are cooking a pork roast we recommend cutting it into 2" thick slabs, this helps them heat through evenly and quickly. However, if you need a whole roast, and it fits into your sous vide machine, you can do it as long as you add some cooking time to account for how long it takes the middle to come up to temperature.

Take the pork and sprinkle it with salt and pepper and seal it into a sous vide pouch. You can also season the meat before sealing it with any normal pork seasoning such as:

- Fresh or dried thyme or rosemary
- Any spice powders such as onion, garlic, paprika, coriander, or cumin
- Chile powders like ancho, chipotle, cayenne
- Marinades
- Sauces like A1 steak sauce, worcester sauce, BBQ sauce, etc.

If adding a sauce or marinade make sure your vacuum sealer does not suck it out. You can normally seal it before all the air is out to prevent this. Also, try to avoid fresh garlic, onions, or ginger, as they can begin to take on a bad flavor over the longer cooking times.

After sealing the pouch place it into the water bath for the indicated cooking time.

Once it's fully cooked remove it from the pouch and pat dry. At this point you can sear the pork in a hot skillet or grill it over high heat to add a nice crust to it. For the roasts you can also apply a normal roast crust such as a garlic paste or horseradish and place it in a very hot oven until the crust sets, about 5 to 10 minutes.

Once the pork is done cooking you can use it as you would a cooked piece of pork. You can also make a nice gravy or pan sauce from the liquid leftover in the sous vide pouch.

Another very convenient use of sous vide is to use it to defrost and cook pork chops that come straight from the freezer. As long as the chop is sealed properly you can take it directly from the freezer and put it in a preheated water bath. Just add 15-30 minutes to the cooking time and it should come out perfectly.

Double Thick Apple Cider Pork Chops

Time: 5 to 12 Hours
Temperature: 131°F / 55°C
Serves: 4

4 extra thick pork chops
8 thyme sprigs
2 apples, sliced
5 tablespoon butter
2 garlic cloves, diced
1 teaspoon sugar
⅔ cup hard apple cider
1 teaspoon cider vinegar
1 tablespoon whole grain mustard

The sweet apples meld perfectly with the cider and mustard to really bring out the flavors of the pork chops. Using sous vide to first cook the pork chops ensures that they'll be perfectly cooked and tender. This dish is great with mashed potatoes or cabbage, or even brussels sprouts and bacon.

Pre-Bath

Preheat the water bath to 131°F / 55°C.

Lightly salt and pepper the pork chops and then seal in the sous vide pouches with the thyme sprigs and butter. Place the pork chops in the water bath and cook for 5 to 12 hours.

Finishing

About 20 minutes before serving you will prepare the sauce. Add 1 tablespoon of butter along with the apples to a pan over medium-high heat. Cook the apples until the juices begin to brown and the apples are beginning to soften.

Remove the pork chops from their pouches, reserving the liquid. Pat the pork chops dry. Quickly sear the pork chops on both sides in a pan over high heat, or on a grill, about 1 or 2 minutes per side.

Finish the sauce while the chops are searing. Add the garlic, sugar, apple cider, cider vinegar, mustard, and about a ½ cup of the juices from the pork chops to the pan with the apples. Simmer for a few minutes until it reaches a sauce-like consistency then serve with the apples on top of the pork chops.

Italian Sausage with Onions and Peppers

Time: 2 to 3 Hours
Temperature: 131°F / 55°C
Serves: 4

8 italian sausage links
1 onion, sliced into ¼" - ½" slices
1 red pepper, cut into ¼" - ½" slices
1 orange pepper, cut into ¼" - ½" slices
1 poblano pepper, cut into ⅛" - ¼" slices
5 garlic cloves, minced
½ cup chicken stock
Salt and pepper

Using sous vide to cook the sausage in this classic dish of sausage and peppers ensures a moist, perfectly cooked sausage. You can also eat this dish on a hoagie roll with melted provolone cheese on top.

Pre-Bath

Preheat the water bath to 131°F / 55°C.

Place the sausage links in the sous vide pouches. Seal the pouches then place in the water bath and cook for 2 to 3 hours.

Finishing

About 15 minutes before the sausage is done start to make the onions and peppers.

Heat some canola oil in a pan over medium heat. Add the onions and salt and pepper them. Cook until they begin to soften, about 5 to 10 minutes. Add the garlic and cook for 2 minutes. Add the peppers and cook for 5 minutes. Add the chicken stock, mix well, and cook until it thickens, about 3 to 4 minutes. Remove from the heat.

Remove the sausage from their pouches and pat them dry. Quickly sear them on two sides in a pan over high heat, or on a grill over high heat, about 1 or 2 minutes per side.

Plate the dish by spooning the peppers and onions onto a plate and topping with 2 sausage links per person. Serve with some warm bread or a baguette.

Pork Roast with Lemon Butter Sauce

Time: 1 to 2 Days
Temperature: 155°F / 68.3°C
Serves: 4 to 6

For the Pork
4-5 pounds boston butt or picnic roast, trimmed
of excess fat
6 sprigs of thyme
6 sprigs of rosemary
2 tablespoons garlic powder
Salt and pepper

For the Sauce
Juices from the pork's sous vide pouch
2 tablespoons flour
1 cup water
½ stick butter
1 tablespoon lemon juice

*The rosemary and thyme help to flavor the pork and
the lemon-butter sauce adds a brightness to the
finished dish. For even more flavor you can brine the
roast ahead of time for about 10 hours or sear it once
it comes out of the water bath. It's great when served
with mashed potatoes and roasted vegetables.*

Pre-Bath

Preheat the water bath to 155°F / 68.3°C.

Prepare the meat by trimming off any excess
fat. This cut of pork can be very fatty but
just focus on removing the large deposits of
fat. Because of the high temperature pork is
cooked at the fat will break down more than
for similar cuts cooked at lower
temperatures.

Salt and pepper the pork roast, then place it
in the pouch with the thyme, rosemary, and
garlic powder. Seal it and place in the water
bath. Let it cook for 1 to 2 days.

Finishing

When you're getting close to serving the
pork you will want to make the sauce. Melt
the butter into a small sauce pan. Whisk
together the flour and the water and then
whisk it into the butter and bring to a boil.
Whisk in the lemon juice and enough of the
juices from the pork roast sous vide pouch
to thin it out to the consistency you want.

Remove the pork roast from the sous vide
pouch and slice into ¾" to 1" slices. Arrange
on a plate and drizzle the lemon-butter
sauce over it.

Jamaican Pork Chops

Time: 3 to 6 Hours
Temperature: 131°F / 55°C
Serves: 4

4 pork chops
⅓ cup dark brown sugar
¼ cup salt
1 tablespoon black pepper
1 tablespoon garlic powder
1 tablespoon onion powder
1 to 3 teaspoons scotch bonnet or habanero chile powder
2 teaspoons dried thyme
1 teaspoon ground coriander
1 teaspoon ground allspice
1 teaspoon cumin
½ teaspoon dried ginger
½ teaspoon ground cinnamon
¼ teaspoon ground cloves
¼ teaspoon ground nutmeg

This recipe is great when served with traditional Jamaican side dishes such as mashed or fried plantains and rice and peas. The heat from the rub really helps to spice up pork chops and other blander cuts like chicken breast or pork tenderloin.

Pre-Bath

Preheat the water bath to 131°F / 55°C.

First make the Jamaican rub by combining all of the ingredients except the pork chops in a bowl and mixing well.

Sprinkle the rub over the pork chops and place them in the sous vide pouches. Seal the pouches then place in the water bath and cook for 3 to 6 hours.

Finishing

Remove the pork chops from their pouches and pat them dry. Quickly sear them on both sides in a pan over high heat, or on a grill over high heat, about 1 or 2 minutes per side. Remove from the heat and serve.

Pulled Pork with Vinegar Sauce

Time: 1 to 2 Days
Temperature: 135°F / 57.2°C
Serves: 5 to 10

For the Pork
4-5 pounds pork shoulder, trimmed of excess fat
1 tablespoon ancho chile powder
1 tablespoon cumin
1 tablespoon coriander
1 tablespoon liquid smoke
1 tablespoon worcester sauce
Salt and pepper

For the Vinegar Sauce
1 cup cider vinegar
¾ cup water
2 tablespoons sugar
1 tablespoon red pepper flakes
2 shallots, diced
2 tablespoons salt
1 teaspoon pepper

This pulled pork can be eaten plain and also makes excellent sandwiches. You can also replace the vinegar sauce with your favorite BBQ sauce for a sweeter meal. I normally serve it with a side of cornbread, coleslaw and some mac and cheese.

Pre-Bath
Preheat the water bath to 135°F / 57.2°C.

Mix the spices together in a bowl. Salt and pepper the pork shoulder, then coat with the spices. Place it in the pouch with the worcester sauce and liquid smoke. Seal the pouch and place in the water bath. Let it cook for 1 to 2 days.

Finishing
When you're getting close to serving the pork you will want to make the sauce. Whisk together all of the ingredients in a bowl.

Remove the pork roast from the sous vide pouch pat dry. Quickly sear the pork on all sides in a pan over high heat, or on a grill, about 1 or 2 minutes per side. Remove from the heat and chop with a knife until in small pieces.

Serve with a spoonful of the vinegar sauce over top.

Chinese 5 Spice Pork Chop

Time: 4 to 8 Hours
Temperature: 131°F / 55°C
Serves: 4

4 pork chops
1 tablespoon soy sauce
2 tablespoons chinese 5 spice powder
1 tablespoon worcester sauce
Salt and pepper

Chinese 5 spice powder adds a lot of great flavor to food. These pork chops are even better when served with some fried rice.

Pre-Bath
Preheat the water bath to 131°F / 55°C.

Lightly salt and pepper the pork chops and sprinkle with the chinese 5 spice powder. Place the pork chops in the sous vide pouches and add the soy sauce and worcester sauce. Seal the sous vide pouches, place in the water bath, and cook for 4 to 8 hours.

Finishing
Remove the pork chops from their pouches, reserving the liquid. Pat the pork chops dry. Quickly sear the pork chops on both sides in a pan over high heat, or on a grill, about 1 or 2 minutes per side. Remove from the heat and serve.

Sweet Red Curry

Time: 3 to 6 Hours
Temperature: 131°F / 55°C
Serves: 4

For the Pork
1 pound pork chop, cut into ¾" chunks
½ tablespoon cumin
1 tablespoon brown sugar
Salt and pepper

For the Curry
1 tablespoon oil
1 onion, diced
2 garlic cloves, diced
2 tablespoons red curry paste
1 ½ cups coconut milk
1 cup water
1 cup corn kernels
1 cup green peas
1 tablespoon fish sauce
1 tablespoon honey
1 tablespoon lime juice
½ cup Thai or italian basil, chopped

This is a classic red curry featuring the pork but it is also great on chicken or lamb. Red curry paste can be found in many supermarkets or ordered online and it is also possible to make your own. Use more or less of it depending on how hot you want your curry.

Pre-Bath
Preheat the water bath to 131°F / 55°C.

Sprinkle the pork chops with the cumin and salt and pepper. Add to the pouches and add the brown sugar. Seal the pouches and cook for 3 to 6 hours.

For the Curry
Heat a pan over medium heat. Add the onion, garlic, and curry paste and stir constantly for about 1 minute. Add coconut milk and water and bring to a boil. Turn down the heat and simmer uncovered for 10 to 15 minutes. Add the the corn and peas and cook for 4 to 6 minutes.

Just before serving stir in the fish sauce, lime juice, and honey.

Finishing
Take the pork out of the pouches and place in a serving dish. Pour the curry on top and garnish with the basil leaves. Serve alongside white or fried rice and with crusty bread or na'an for soaking up the curry.

Pork Chop Sandwich with Slaw

Time: 2 to 8 Hours
Temperature: 131°F / 55°C
Serves: 4

For the Pork
4 pork chops
½ teaspoon paprika
½ teaspoon garlic powder
½ teaspoon onion powder
½ teaspoon ancho chile powder
Salt and pepper

For the Slaw
2 cups cabbage
1 cup carrot, shredded
1 tablespoon apple cider vinegar
1 tablespoon dijon mustard
2 tablespoons olive oil

4 sandwich rolls
4 slices cheddar cheese
4 dill pickles

If you want to add some heat to the sandwich you can add red pepper flakes or tabasco sauce to the coleslaw. These pork chop sandwiches are also very good with macaroni and cheese or a cold pasta salad.

Pre-Bath
Preheat the water bath to 131°F / 55°C.

Mix the spices together in a bowl. Salt and pepper the pork chops then sprinkle with the spice mixture. Seal in sous vide pouches, place in the water bath, and cook for 2 to 8 hours.

Finishing
Preheat the broiler on the oven.

In a large bowl whisk together the mustard and the vinegar. Slowly whisk in the olive oil. Add the cabbage and carrots and mix well.

Remove the pork chops from the water bath and pat dry. Sear the pork chops on a hot grill or in a hot pan, about 1 or 2 minutes per side.

Place the pork chops on a roasting sheet. Cover the top of the pork chops with the cheese. Place the buns on the sheet with the cut side up. Place the whole roasting sheet under the broiler until the cheese melts and the buns begin to brown.

Remove the sheet from the oven, place the pork chops on top of the buns, top with the coleslaw and serve.

"Falling Off the Bone" Ribs

Time: 8 to 12 Hours
Temperature: 135°F / 57.2°C
Serves: 2 to 4

2 pounds of back or baby back ribs
1 tablespoon celery salt
1 tablespoon paprika
½ tablespoon garlic powder
½ tablespoon freshly ground black pepper
½ tablespoon ancho chile powder

These ribs are simple to make and very flavorful. You can also glaze them with BBQ sauce when you are searing them for even more flavor.

Pre-Bath

Preheat the water bath to 135°F / 57.2°C.

In a bowl mix together all the spices. Cut the ribs into pieces that will easily fit into your sous vide bags. Sprinkle salt on the ribs and then coat them with ½ of the spice mix.

Place the ribs into the sous vide pouches and then seal. Be sure you don't seal the ribs too tightly or the bones may pierce the bag. Place in the water bath and cook for 8 to 12 hours, until they are very tender.

Finishing

Preheat a grill to very high heat.

Remove the sous vide pouches from the water bath and take the ribs out of the sous vide pouches. Pat them dry and then sprinkle the meaty side with the remaining spice rub.

Quickly grill the ribs just until the meat is seared, about 1 to 2 minutes per side. Take off the grill and serve.

Pork Loin with Olive Tapenade

Time: 4 to 8 Hours
Temperature: 131°F / 55°C
Serves: 4

For the Pork
1 to 2 pounds pork loin roast
1 teaspoon garlic powder
1 teaspoon paprika
½ teaspoon cumin
Salt and pepper

For the Olive Tapenade
1 cup kalamata olives, pitted
2 anchovy filets or 1 tablespoon capers
2 garlic cloves
¼ teaspoon red pepper flakes
1 tablespoon fresh parsley, chopped
2 tablespoons balsamic or red wine vinegar
3 tablespoons olive oil
Salt and pepper

The saltiness of the olives and anchovies helps bring out the flavor of the pork. This dish is great when served with roasted tomatoes or vegetables, or even a crisp salad. This tapenade is also very good with steak or lamb.

Pre-Bath
Preheat the water bath to 131°F / 55°C.

In a bowl mix together the garlic powder, paprika and cumin. Salt and pepper the pork and then sprinkle the spice mix over top. Add to the sous vide pouch and seal. Place in the water bath and cook for 4 to 8 hours.

Finishing
About 5 minutes before the pork is done make the olive tapenade. Put all of the tapenade ingredients into a food processor and pulse several times until it forms a coarse puree.

Remove the pork from the water bath and pat dry. Sear the pork on a very hot grill or in a hot pan, about 1 to 2 minutes per side. Remove from the heat and place on a plate. Spoon the tapenade across the top of the pork loin and serve.

Turkey

Overcooked, bland, and dried out turkey is very common around homes. With practice it is possible to cook turkey perfectly using traditional methods but it is always a fine line between perfect and overcooked. Using sous vide always results in uniformly tender turkey that is very moist.

Unlike some other ingredients where sous vide can radically change the ingredient, cooking turkey meat sous vide is mainly an act of convenience and consistency.

I often use sous vide turkey as a basis for other dishes such as hot turkey sandwiches, turkey cutlets, or turkey cold cuts. And of course it is great plain with some gravy made from the liquids in the bag.

Time and Temperature Guidelines

The FDA states that turkey is safe when it is held at 136°F for over 63 minutes, or 140°F for over 30 minutes. This is very easy to do with sous vide and almost impossible to do with traditional methods.

However, even though it is possible to cook turkey at temperature below 140°F we have found that the texture is very different and tastes "raw". To avoid this we recommend turkey breasts cooked at 140°F to 147°F for 1 to 4 hours and legs or thighs cooked at 147°F for 4 to 8 hours.

Basic Process

Sous vide turkey is one of the easiest and fastest applications of sous vide cooking that there is. It helps if the turkey is no longer whole, as the smaller pieces will heat more quickly and evenly.

Preheat your sous vide machine to the temperature desired, we recommend 140°F to 147°F for most cuts but feel free to experiment within the safety guidelines above 136°F.

Seal the meat in a sous vide pouch with salt and pepper and other spices such as rosemary, sage, thyme, butter, or other seasonings you like.

After sealing the pouch place it into the water bath for the indicated cooking time.

Once it's fully cooked remove it from the pouch and pat dry. At this point you can sear the meat in a hot skillet to add a nice crust to it or you can slice it and serve as is. You can also make a great gravy or pan sauce from the liquids in the bag.

Turkey skin that was in the pouch will not become crispy due to the moisture present in sous vide cooking. The best solution to this is to take it off of the bird before cooking the meat sous vide.

As you get close to serving time, you can manually crisp the turkey skin. There are many methods that work, using a hot skillet with a little oil is normally quick. You can also brown it on a baking sheet in the oven set to 375°F but make sure you use one with raised edges to prevent fat from falling into the oven.

Turkey Breast and Avocado Salad

Time: 1 to 4 Hours
Temperature: 147°F / 63.9°C
Serves: 4

For the Turkey
1 pound turkey breast or filets
½ teaspoon garlic powder
½ teaspoon onion powder
Salt and pepper

Arugula and Avocado Salad Ingredients
7 cups arugula or baby spinach
1 avocado, sliced
Parmigiano-Reggiano Cheese, for shaving

Lemon Vinaigrette Ingredients
2 tablespoons lemon juice
1 garlic clove, minced
⅓ cup olive oil
Salt and pepper

This is a nice and light salad with the bite of the arugula being offset by the richness of the avocado. This salad is great for a whole meal, especially if you serve it with warm rolls or a fresh baguette.

Pre-Bath
Preheat the water bath to 147°F / 63.9°C.

Salt and pepper the turkey breast filets then sprinkle with the paprika and chipotle pepper powder. Seal in sous vide pouches, place in the water bath and cook for 1 to 4 hours.

Finishing
Remove the turkey breasts from the water bath and pat dry.

Now make the vinaigrette. Combine the lemon juice and garlic in a bowl, add some salt and pepper and let sit for a few minutes. Slowly whisk in olive oil until the mixture thickens.

Sear the breasts on a very hot grill or in a hot pan, about 1 minute per side. Remove from the heat and cut into strips.

Place the arugula in a serving bowl and add enough vinaigrette to flavor it, tossing to mix. Top the arugula with the avocado slices and chicken. Spoon a bit more dressing over them and season with salt and pepper. Using a vegetable peeler, shave strips of Parmesan cheese over the top and serve.

Smoky Turkey Burger

Time: 1 to 4 Hours
Temperature: 147°F / 63.9°C
Serves: 4

4 turkey breast filets
½ teaspoon paprika
¼ teaspoon chipotle pepper powder
Salt and pepper
½ onion, thickly sliced
10 mushrooms, thickly sliced
½ cup BBQ sauce
4 sandwich rolls
4 slices smoked gouda or smoked provolone cheese
4 dill pickles

The turkey is a great base for the mushrooms and onion and the BBQ sauce adds some sweetness and a little kick. These turkey burgers are great with normal burger accompaniments such as chips or fries and potato salad.

Pre-Bath
Preheat the water bath to 147°F / 63.9°C.

Salt and pepper the turkey breast filets then sprinkle with the paprika and chipotle pepper powder. Seal in sous vide pouches, place in the water bath and cook for 1 to 4 hours.

Finishing
Preheat the broiler on the oven.

Add some canola or olive oil to a pan set over medium heat and warm. Add the onions and mushrooms, stirring occasionally, until they are soft. Stir in the BBQ sauce and set aside.

Remove the turkey breasts from the water bath and pat dry. Place the turkey on a roasting sheet. Cover the top of the turkey with the onions and mushrooms mixture and top with the cheese. Place the buns on the sheet with the cut side up. Place the whole roasting sheet under the broiler until the cheese melts and the buns begin to brown.

Remove the sheet from the oven, place the turkey on top of the buns and serve with the dill pickles.

Panang Curry with Turkey

Time: 4 to 8 Hours
Temperature: 145°F / 62.7°C
Serves: 4

1 pound turkey legs and thighs, cut in bite-sized pieces
1 tablespoon oil
1 large onion, chopped
1 to 2 tablespoons Panang curry paste
1 cup coconut milk
¼ cup heavy cream
2 tablespoons lime juice
1 tablespoon fish sauce
1 tablespoon brown sugar
½ cup roasted peanuts, chopped
½ cup basil leaves, chopped
1 cup pineapple, chopped

This is a nice and creamy curry. If you want more heat you can always add cayenne pepper or tabasco sauce. It's best when served with rice or bread to soak up the flavors. You can also use green or red curry paste if you cannot find the Panang curry.

Pre-Bath
Preheat the water bath to 145°F / 62.7°C.

Salt and pepper the turkey and add to the sous vide pouches. Seal the pouches and place them in the water bath and cook for 4 to 8 hours.

Finishing
About 20 minutes before the turkey is done begin working on the curry.

Heat the oil in a pan over medium heat. Add the onions and curry paste and stir for 3 minutes. Add the coconut milk and bring to a simmer. Reduce the heat and cook for 15 minutes, until it is reduced and thick.

Remove the turkey from the sous vide pouches and set aside. Add some of the juices from the pouch to the pan and simmer for 5 more minutes. Add the turkey, heavy cream, fish sauce, lime juice and brown sugar and stir well. Cook for 5 minutes more. Stir in the peanuts, basil and pineapple.

Serve with rice or crusty bread on the side.

Pesto Turkey Breast Salad

Time: 1 to 4 Hours
Temperature: 147°F / 63.9°C
Serves: 4

For the Turkey
2 turkey breasts or filets, cut into half
½ teaspoon garlic powder
½ teaspoon dried basil
Salt and pepper

5 bacon strips, cut lengthwise ½" wide
¼ cup mayonnaise
5 tablespoons pesto
½ pint cherry tomatoes, halved
½ loaf of bread, preferably a baguette or
sourdough
2 tablespoons olive oil
1 teaspoon garlic, minced
Salt and pepper

This is a very flavorful meal, getting a lot of complex flavors from the pesto and the homemade croutons. It's hearty enough to be served as a main course, especially if you add some romaine or bibb lettuce to it.

Pre-Bath
Preheat the water bath to 147°F / 63.9°C.

Salt and pepper the turkey breasts then sprinkle with the garlic powder and the dried basil. Seal in sous vide pouches, place in the water bath and cook for 1 to 4 hours.

Finishing
When the turkey is almost done, assemble the rest of the dish.

Preheat the oven to 350°F. Cut the loaf of bread into ½" to 1" cubes. Toss the cubes with olive oil, garlic, salt and pepper then place on a baking sheet with raised sides and toast them in the oven for 10 to 15 minutes. The cubes should be slightly crispy and browned but still soft on the inside. Once done remove from the oven and set aside.

Fry the bacon in a pan over medium heat until the fat is rendered and they turn crisp. Remove from the heat and drain on paper towels.

Remove the turkey breasts from the water bath and pat dry. Sear the breasts on a very hot grill or in a hot pan, about 1 minute per side. Remove from the heat and cut into strips.

Whisk together the mayonnaise and pesto in a bowl.

Place the turkey on individual serving plates. Spoon a decent amount of the mayonnaise pesto mixture on top. Top with the tomatoes, croutons and bacon strips and serve.

Turkey and Avocado Roll

Time: 1 to 4 Hours
Temperature: 147°F / 63.9°C
Serves: 2

2 turkey breast filets
2 sandwich rolls
1 avocado, sliced
1 red pepper, sliced
2 slices provolone cheese
Honey Mustard
Mayonnaise

Turkey and avocado go great together because the avocado adds a richness that turkey normally lacks. These are very simple sandwiches to put together but have a great flavor.

Pre-Bath

Preheat the water bath to 147°F / 63.9°C.

Salt and pepper the turkey breast filets and seal in sous vide pouches. Place in the water bath and cook for 1 to 4 hours.

Finishing

Remove the turkey breasts from the water bath and pat dry. Sear the breasts on a very hot grill or in a hot pan, about 1 minute per side. Remove from the heat, assemble the sandwich, and serve.

Turkey and Coleslaw

Time: 1 to 4 Hours
Temperature: 147°F / 63.9°C
Serves: 4

For the Turkey
2 turkey breasts or filets, cut in half
1 teaspoon ginger powder
Salt and pepper

For the Coleslaw
3 cups red cabbage, thinly sliced
1 red bell pepper, thinly sliced
1 cup snow pea pods, cut into strips
2 large carrots, peeled and cut into matchsticks
2 tablespoons sesame seeds, toasted

For the Vinaigrette
1 ½ tablespoons lemon juice
1 ½ tablespoons rice wine vinegar
1 tablespoon soy sauce
1 ½ teaspoons fresh ginger, minced
3 teaspoons honey
Salt and pepper
3 tablespoons peanut oil
1 tablespoon sesame oil

The coleslaw helps add a nice texture and bold Asian flavors to the turkey.

Pre-Bath
Preheat the water bath to 147°F / 63.9°C.

Salt and pepper the turkey breast filets then sprinkle with the ginger powder. Seal in sous vide pouches, place in the water bath and cook for 1 to 4 hours.

Finishing
When the turkey is almost done, assemble the rest of the dish.

Combine the shredded red cabbage, red bell pepper, carrots, and snow peas in a large bowl.

In a small bowl mix together the lemon juice, vinegar, soy sauce, ginger, honey, and salt and pepper. Let sit for a few minutes. Slowly whisk in the peanut and sesame oil. Dress the coleslaw, tasting as you go for seasoning.

Remove the turkey breasts from the water bath and pat dry. Sear the breasts on a very hot grill or in a hot pan, about 1 minute per side. Remove from the heat.

Place the turkey on individual plates and top with a large spoonful of the coleslaw. Garnish with the sesame seeds and serve.

Turkey Breast with Herb Butter

Time: 1 to 4 Hours
Temperature: 147°F / 63.9°C
Serves: 4

For the Turkey
1 to 2 pounds turkey breast
1 teaspoon dried thyme
1 teaspoon garlic powder
Salt and pepper

For the Butter
1 stick butter, softened at room temperature
1 tablespoon fresh thyme
2 tablespoons fresh basil, chopped
½ tablespoon fresh sage, chopped
⅛ teaspoon ground black pepper

This butter topping adds some great richness to the normally lean turkey. It also adds a lot of flavor with the herbs. You can serve this turkey with a side of rice and steamed vegetables for a healthy, complete meal.

Pre-Bath
Preheat the water bath to 147°F / 63.9°C.

Salt and pepper the turkey then add to the sous vide pouches. Add the garlic powder and dried thyme and then seal and place in the water bath. Cook the turkey for 1 to 4 hours.

Finishing
To make the butter place all of the butter ingredients in a bowl and mix and mash thoroughly using a fork.

Take the turkey out of the pouches and pat dry. Sear it on a very hot grill or in a hot pan, about 1 to 2 minutes per side. Place the turkey on a plate and place a spoonful or two of the butter on top.

Turkey Leg with Cranberry BBQ Sauce

Time: 4 to 8 Hours
Temperature: 145°F / 62.7°C
Serves: 4

For the Turkey
1 to 2 pounds turkey legs and thighs
1 teaspoon dried thyme
1 teaspoon garlic powder
Salt and pepper

For the BBQ Sauce
1 ½ cups ketchup
3 tablespoons Worcester sauce
¼ cup apple cider vinegar
2 tablespoons yellow mustard
1 tablespoon onion powder
2 tablespoons molasses
⅓ cup cranberry sauce
½ teaspoon mustard powder
Salt and pepper

The cranberry BBQ sauce is a nice twist on a classic Thanksgiving flavor combination. It's great when served with a chunky stuffing or mashed potatoes.

Pre-Bath
Preheat the water bath to 145°F / 62.7°C.

Salt and pepper the turkey then add to the sous vide pouches. Add the garlic powder and dried thyme and then seal and place in the water bath. Cook the turkey for 4 to 8 hours.

Finishing
Start the BBQ sauce at least 30 to 40 minutes before you want to eat. You can also make it ahead of time and save it in the refrigerator for several months.

Place all of the BBQ sauce ingredients into a pan set over medium-high heat and bring to a boil, stirring regularly to make sure all of the ingredients meld together. Reduce the heat and simmer, stirring regularly, for around 20 minutes until it thickens.

Take the turkey out of the pouches and pat dry. Sear them on a very hot grill or in a hot pan, about 1 to 2 minutes per side. Place the turkey on a plate and place a spoonful or two of the BBQ sauce on top.

Time and Temperature Charts

One of the most interesting aspects of sous vide cooking is how much the time and temperature used can change the texture of the food. Many people experiment with different cooking times and temperatures to tweak dishes various ways.

The numbers below are merely beginning recommendations and are a good place to start. Feel free to increase or lower the temperature several degrees or play around with the cooking time as you see fit as long as you stay in the safe-zone discussed in each chapter.

You can also get this time and temperature information
on your mobile phone if you have an iPhone, iPad or an Android.

Just search for "Sous Vide" and look for the guide by "Primolicious".

Beef - Roasts and Tough Cuts

Bottom Round Roast
Medium Rare   131°F for 2 to 3 Days (55.0°C)
Medium   140°F for 2 to 3 Days (60.0°C)
Well-Traditional 160°F for 1 to 2 Days (71.1°C)

Brisket
Medium Rare   131°F for 2 to 3 Days (55.0°C)
Medium   140°F for 2 to 3 Days (60.0°C)
Well-Traditional 160°F for 1 to 2 Days (71.1°C)

Cheek
Medium Rare   131°F for 2 to 3 Days (55.0°C)
Medium   149°F for 2 to 3 Days (65.0°C)
Well-Traditional 160°F for 1 to 2 Days (71.1°C)

Chuck Roast
Medium Rare   131°F for 2 to 3 Days (55.0°C)
Medium   140°F for 2 to 3 Days (60.0°C)
Well-Traditional 160°F for 1 to 2 Days (71.1°C)

Pot Roast
Medium Rare   131°F for 2 to 3 Days (55.0°C)
Medium   140°F for 2 to 3 Days (60.0°C)
Well-Traditional 160°F for 1 to 2 Days (71.1°C)

Prime Rib Roast
Medium Rare   131°F for 5 to 10 Hours (55°C)
Medium   140°F for 5 to 10 Hours (60°C)

Rib Eye Roast
Medium Rare   131°F for 5 to 10 Hours (55°C)
Medium   140°F for 5 to 10 Hours (60°C)

Ribs
Medium Rare   131°F for 2 to 3 Days (55.0°C)
Medium   140°F for 2 to 3 Days (60.0°C)
Well-Traditional 160°F for 1 to 2 Days (71.1°C)

Shank
Medium Rare   131°F for 2 to 3 Days (55.0°C)
Medium   140°F for 2 to 3 Days (60.0°C)
Well-Traditional 160°F for 1 to 2 Days (71.1°C)

Short Ribs
Medium Rare   131°F for 2 to 3 Days (55.0°C)
Medium   140°F for 2 to 3 Days (60.0°C)
Well-Traditional 160°F for 1 to 2 Days (71.1°C)

Sirloin Roast
Medium Rare   131°F for 5 to 10 Hours (55.0°C)
Medium   140°F for 5 to 10 Hours (60.0°C)

Stew Meat
Medium Rare   131°F for 4 to 8 Hours (55.0°C)
Medium   140°F for 4 to 8 Hours (60.0°C)

Sweetbreads
Medium   140°F for 30 to 45 Min (60°C)
Pre-Roasting   152°F for 60 Min (66.7°C)

Tenderloin Roast
Medium Rare   131°F for 3 to 6 Hours (55.0°C)
Medium   140°F for 3 to 6 Hours (60.0°C)

Tongue
Low and Slow   140°F for 48 Hours (60.0°C)
High and Fast 158°F for 24 Hours (70.0°C)

Top Loin Strip Roast
Medium Rare   131°F for 4 to 8 Hours (55.0°C)
Medium   140°F for 4 to 8 Hours (60.0°C)

Top Round Roast
Medium Rare   131°F for 1 to 3 Days (55.0°C)
Medium   140°F for 1 to 3 Days (60.0°C)
Well-Traditional 160°F for 1 to 2 Days (71.1°C)

Tri-Tip Roast
Medium Rare   131°F for 5 to 10 Hours (55°C)
Medium   140°F for 5 to 10 Hours (60°C)

Beef - Steak and Tender Cuts

Blade Steak

Medium Rare	131°F for 4 to 10 Hours (55.0°C)
Medium	140°F for 4 to 10 Hours (60.0°C)

Bottom Round Steak

Medium Rare	131°F for 1 to 3 Days (55.0°C)
Medium	140°F for 1 to 3 Days (60.0°C)

Chuck Steak

Medium Rare	131°F for 1 to 2 Days (55.0°C)
Medium	140°F for 1 to 2 Days (60.0°C)

Eye Round Steak

Medium Rare	131°F for 1 to 2 Days (55.0°C)
Medium	140°F for 1 to 2 Days (60.0°C)

Flank Steak

Medium Rare	131°F for 2 to 12 Hours (55.0°C)
Medium Rare and Tender	131°F for 1 to 2 Days (55.0°C)
Medium	140°F for 2 to 12 Hours (60.0°C)
Medium and Tender	140°F for 1 to 2 Days (60.0°C)

Flat Iron Steak

Medium Rare	131°F for 4 to 10 Hours (55.0°C)
Medium	140°F for 4 to 10 Hours (60.0°C)

Hamburger

Medium Rare	131°F for 2 to 4 Hours (55.0°C)
Medium	140°F for 2 to 4 Hours (60.0°C)

Hanger Steak

Medium Rare	131°F for 2 to 3 Hours (55.0°C)
Medium	140°F for 2 to 3 Hours (60.0°C)

Porterhouse Steak

Medium Rare	131°F for 2 to 3 Hours (55.0°C)
Medium	140°F for 2 to 3 Hours (60.0°C)

Rib Steak

Medium Rare	131°F for 2 to 8 Hours (55.0°C)
Medium	140°F for 2 to 8 Hours (60.0°C)

Ribeye Steak

Medium Rare	131°F for 2 to 8 Hours (55.0°C)
Medium	140°F for 2 to 8 Hours (60.0°C)

Sausage

Medium Rare	131°F for 2 to 3 Hours (55.0°C)
Medium	140°F for 90 to 120 Min (60°C)

Shoulder Steak

Medium Rare	131°F for 4 to 10 Hours (55.0°C)
Medium	140°F for 4 to 10 Hours (60.0°C)

Sirloin Steak

Medium Rare	131°F for 2 to 10 Hours (55.0°C)
Medium	140°F for 2 to 10 Hours (60.0°C)

Skirt Steak

Medium Rare	131°F for 1 to 2 Days (55.0°C)
Medium	140°F for 1 to 2 Days (60.0°C)

T-Bone Steak

Medium Rare	131°F for 2 to 3 Hours (55.0°C)
Medium	140°F for 2 to 3 Hours (60.0°C)

Tenderloin Steak

Medium Rare	131°F for 2 to 3 Hours (55.0°C)
Medium	140°F for 2 to 3 Hours (60.0°C)

Top Loin Strip Steak

Medium Rare	131°F for 2 to 3 Hours (55.0°C)
Medium	140°F for 2 to 3 Hours (60.0°C)

Top Round Steak

Medium Rare	131°F for 1 to 2 Days (55.0°C)
Medium	140°F for 1 to 2 Days (60.0°C)

Tri-Tip Steak

Medium Rare	131°F for 2 to 10 Hours (55.0°C)
Medium	140°F for 2 to 10 Hours (60.0°C)

Chicken and Eggs

Breast
Rare   136°F for 1 to 4 Hours (57.8°C)
Medium / Typical   140°F - 147°F for 1 to 4 Hours (63.9°C)

Drumstick
Rare   140°F for 90 to 120 Min (60.0°C)
Ideal   148°F - 156°F for 2 to 5 Hours (64.4°C)
For Shredding   160°F - 170°F for 8 to 12 Hours (71.1°C)

Eggs
Over Easy   142°F - 146°F for 45 to 60 Min (62.8°C)
Poached   142°F for 45 to 60 Min (61.1°C)
Perfect   148°F for 45 to 60 Min (64.4°C)
Hard Boiled   149°F - 152°F for 45 to 60 Min (65.6°C)
Pasteurized   135°F for 75 Min (57.2°C)

Leg
Rare   140°F for 90 to 120 Min (60.0°C)
Ideal   148°F - 156°F for 2 to 5 Hours (64.4°C)
For Shredding   160°F - 170°F for 8 to 12 Hours (71.1°C)

Sausage
White Meat   140°F for 1 to 2 Hours (63.9°C)
Mixed Meat   140°F for 90 to 120 Min (60.0°C)

Thigh
Rare   140°F for 90 to 120 Min (60.0°C)
Ideal   148°F - 156°F for 2 to 5 Hours (64.4°C)
For Shredding   160°F - 170°F for 8 to 12 Hours (71.1°C)

Whole Chicken
Rare   140°F for 4 to 6 Hours (60.0°C)
Typical   148°F for 4 to 6 Hours (64.4°C)
Larger   148°F for 6 to 8 Hours (64.4°C)
Butterflied   148°F for 2 to 4 Hours (64.4°C)

Duck

Breast

Medium-Rare	131°F for 2 to 4 Hours (55.0°C)
Medium	140°F for 2 to 4 Hours (60.0°C)

Drumstick

Medium-Rare	131°F for 3 to 6 Hours (55.0°C)
Well	176°F for 8 to 10 Hours (80.0°C)
Confit	167°F for 10 to 20 Hours (75.0°C)

Foie Gras

Foie Gras	134°F for 35 to 55 Min (56.7°C)

Leg

Medium-Rare	131°F for 3 to 6 Hours (55.0°C)
Well	176°F for 8 to 10 Hours (80.0°C)
Duck Confit	167°F for 10 to 20 Hours (75.0°C)

Sausage

Breast Meat	131°F for 1 to 2 Hours (55.0°C)
Mixed Meat	131°F for 2 to 3 Hours (55.0°C)

Thigh

Medium-Rare	131°F for 3 to 6 Hours (55.0°C)
Well	176°F for 8 to 10 Hours (80.0°C)
Confit	167°F for 10 to 20 Hours (75.0°C)

Whole Duck

Medium-Rare	131°F for 3 to 6 Hours (55.0°C)
Medium	140°F for 3 to 6 Hours (60.0°C)
Confit	167°F for 10 to 20 Hours (75.0°C)

Fish and Shellfish

Arctic Char

"Sushi", Rare	104°F for 10 to 30 Min (40.0°C)
"Sushi", Medium Rare	122°F for 10 to 30 Min (50.0°C)
Medium Rare	132°F for 10 to 30 Min (55.6°C)
Medium	140°F for 10 to 30 Min (60.0°C)

Bass

"Sushi", Rare	104°F for 10 to 30 Min (40.0°C)
"Sushi", Medium Rare	122°F for 10 to 30 Min (50.0°C)
Medium Rare	132°F for 10 to 30 Min (55.6°C)
Medium	140°F for 10 to 30 Min (60.0°C)

Black Sea Bass

"Sushi", Rare	104°F for 10 to 30 Min (40.0°C)
"Sushi", Medium Rare	122°F for 10 to 30 Min (50.0°C)
Medium Rare	132°F for 10 to 30 Min (55.6°C)
Medium	140°F for 10 to 30 Min (60.0°C)

Bluefish

"Sushi", Medium Rare	122°F for 10 to 30 Min (50.0°C)
Medium Rare	132°F for 10 to 30 Min (55.6°C)
Medium	140°F for 10 to 30 Min (60.0°C)

Carp

"Sushi", Medium Rare	122°F for 10 to 30 Min (50.0°C)
Medium Rare	132°F for 10 to 30 Min (55.6°C)
Medium	140°F for 10 to 30 Min (60.0°C)

Catfish

"Sushi", Medium Rare	122°F for 10 to 30 Min (50.0°C)
Medium Rare	132°F for 10 to 30 Min (55.6°C)
Medium	140°F for 10 to 30 Min (60.0°C)

Cod

Rare	104°F for 10 to 30 Min (40.0°C)
"Sushi", Medium Rare	129°F for 10 to 30 Min (53.9°C)
Medium Rare	132°F for 10 to 30 Min (55.6°C)

Flounder

"Sushi", Medium Rare	122°F for 10 to 30 Min (50.0°C)
Medium Rare	132°F for 10 to 30 Min (55.6°C)
Medium	140°F for 10 to 30 Min (60.0°C)

Grouper

"Sushi", Rare	104°F for 10 to 30 Min (40.0°C)
"Sushi", Medium Rare	122°F for 10 to 30 Min (50.0°C)
Medium Rare	132°F for 10 to 30 Min (55.6°C)
Medium	140°F for 10 to 30 Min (60.0°C)

Haddock

"Sushi", Medium Rare	122°F for 10 to 30 Min (50.0°C)
Medium Rare	132°F for 10 to 30 Min (55.6°C)
Medium	140°F for 10 to 30 Min (60.0°C)

Hake

"Sushi", Rare	104°F for 10 to 30 Min (40.0°C)
"Sushi", Medium Rare	122°F for 10 to 30 Min (50.0°C)
Medium Rare	132°F for 10 to 30 Min (55.6°C)
Medium	140°F for 10 to 30 Min (60.0°C)

Halibut

"Sushi", Rare	104°F for 10 to 30 Min (40.0°C)
"Sushi", Medium Rare	129°F for 10 to 30 Min (53.9°C)
Medium Rare	132°F for 10 to 30 Min (55.6°C)
Medium	140°F for 10 to 30 Min (60.0°C)

King Crab Tail

King Crab Tail	140°F for 30 to 45 Min (60.0°C)

Lobster

Medium Rare	126°F for 15 to 40 Min (52.2°C)
Medium	140°F for 15 to 40 Min (60.0°C)

Mackerel

"Sushi", Rare	109°F for 10 to 30 Min (42.8°C)
"Sushi", Medium Rare	122°F for 10 to 30 Min (50.0°C)
Medium Rare	132°F for 10 to 30 Min (55.6°C)

Mahi Mahi

"Sushi", Medium Rare	122°F for 10 to 30 Min (50.0°C)
Medium Rare	132°F for 10 to 30 Min (55.6°C)
Medium	140°F for 10 to 30 Min (60.0°C)

Marlin

"Sushi", Rare	104°F for 10 to 30 Min (40.0°C)
"Sushi", Medium Rare	122°F for 10 to 30 Min (50.0°C)
Medium Rare	132°F for 10 to 30 Min (55.6°C)
Medium	140°F for 10 to 30 Min (60.0°C)

Monkfish

"Sushi", Rare	104°F for 10 to 30 Min (40.0°C)
"Sushi", Medium Rare	118°F for 10 to 30 Min (47.8°C)
Medium Rare	132°F for 10 to 30 Min (55.6°C)
Medium	140°F for 10 to 30 Min (60.0°C)

Octopus

Slow Cook	170°F for 4 to 7 Hours (76.7°C)
Fast Cook	180°F for 2 to 3 Hours (82.2°C)

Red Snapper

"Sushi", Rare	104°F for 10 to 30 Min (40.0°C)
"Sushi", Medium Rare	122°F for 10 to 30 Min (50.0°C)
Medium Rare	132°F for 10 to 30 Min (55.6°C)
Medium	140°F for 10 to 30 Min (60.0°C)

Salmon

"Sushi", Rare	104°F for 10 to 30 Min (40.0°C)
"Sushi", Medium Rare	122°F for 10 to 30 Min (50.0°C)
Medium Rare	132°F for 10 to 30 Min (55.6°C)
Medium	140°F for 10 to 30 Min (60.0°C)

Sardines

"Sushi", Rare	104°F for 10 to 30 Min (40.0°C)
"Sushi", Medium Rare	122°F for 10 to 30 Min (50.0°C)
Medium Rare	132°F for 10 to 30 Min (55.6°C)
Medium	140°F for 10 to 30 Min (60.0°C)

Scallops

Pre-Sear	122°F for 15 to 35 Min (50.0°C)

Scrod

"Sushi", Medium Rare	122°F for 10 to 30 Min (50.0°C)
Medium Rare	132°F for 10 to 30 Min (55.6°C)
Medium	140°F for 10 to 30 Min (60.0°C)

Sea Bass

"Sushi", Rare	104°F for 10 to 30 Min (40.0°C)
"Sushi", Medium Rare	122°F for 10 to 30 Min (50.0°C)
Medium Rare	132°F for 10 to 30 Min (55.6°C)
Medium	140°F for 10 to 30 Min (60.0°C)

Shark

"Sushi", Medium Rare	122°F for 10 to 30 Min (50.0°C)
Medium Rare	132°F for 10 to 30 Min (55.6°C)
Medium	140°F for 10 to 30 Min (60.0°C)

Shrimp

"Sushi" Medium Rare	122°F for 15 to 35 Min (50.0°C)
Medium Rare	132°F for 15 to 35 Min (55.6°C)

Skate

"Sushi", Medium Rare	129°F for 10 to 30 Min (53.9°C)
Medium Rare	132°F for 10 to 30 Min (55.6°C)
Medium	140°F for 10 to 30 Min (60.0°C)

Soft Shell Crab

Standard	145°F for 3 hours (62.8°C)

Sole

"Sushi", Medium Rare	122°F for 10 to 30 Min (50.0°C)
Medium Rare	132°F for 10 to 30 Min (55.6°C)
Medium	143°F for 10 to 30 Min (61.7°C)

Squid

Pre-Sear	113°F for 45 to 60 Min (45.0°C)
Low Heat	138°F for 2 to 4 Hours (58.9°C)
High Heat	180°F for 1 Hour (82.2°C)

Striped Bass

"Sushi", Rare	104°F for 10 to 30 Min (40.0°C)
"Sushi", Medium Rare	122°F for 10 to 30 Min (50.0°C)
Medium Rare	132°F for 10 to 30 Min (55.6°C)
Medium	140°F for 10 to 30 Min (60.0°C)

Sturgeon

"Sushi", Rare	104°F for 10 to 30 Min (40.0°C)
"Sushi", Medium Rare	122°F for 10 to 30 Min (50.0°C)
Medium Rare	132°F for 10 to 30 Min (55.6°C)
Medium	140°F for 10 to 30 Min (60.0°C)

Swordfish

"Sushi", Rare	104°F for 10 to 30 Min (40.0°C)
"Sushi", Medium Rare	122°F for 10 to 30 Min (50.0°C)
Medium Rare	132°F for 10 to 30 Min (55.6°C)
Medium	140°F for 10 to 30 Min (60.0°C)

Tilapia

"Sushi", Rare	104°F for 10 to 30 Min (40.0°C)
"Sushi", Medium Rare	122°F for 10 to 30 Min (50.0°C)
Medium Rare	132°F for 10 to 30 Min (55.6°C)
Medium	140°F for 10 to 30 Min (60.0°C)

Trout

"Sushi", Medium Rare	122°F for 10 to 30 Min (50.0°C)
Medium Rare	132°F for 10 to 30 Min (55.6°C)
Medium	140°F for 10 to 30 Min (60.0°C)

Tuna

"Sushi", Rare	100°F for 10 to 20 Min (37.8°C)
"Sushi", Medium Rare	129°F for 10 to 30 Min (53.9°C)
Medium Rare	132°F for 10 to 30 Min (55.6°C)

Turbot

"Sushi", Medium Rare	129°F for 10 to 30 Min (53.9°C)
Medium Rare	132°F for 10 to 30 Min (55.6°C)
Medium	140°F for 10 to 30 Min (60.0°C)

Fruits and Vegetables

Acorn Squash	183°F for 1 to 2 Hours (83.9°C)		**Pears**	183°F for 25 to 35 Min (83.9°C)
Apples	183°F for 25 to 40 Min (83.9°C)		**Pineapple**	167°F for 45 to 60 Min (75.0°C)
Artichokes	183°F for 45 to 75 Min (83.9°C)		**Plums**	167°F for 15 to 20 Min (75.0°C)
Asparagus	183°F for 30 to 40 Min (83.9°C)		**Potatoes**	
Banana	183°F for 10 to 15 Min (83.9°C)		Small	183°F for 30 to 60 Min (83.9°C)
Beet	183°F for 30 to 60 Min (83.9°C)		Large	183°F for 60 to 120 Min (83.9°C)
Broccoli	183°F for 20 to 30 Min (83.9°C)		**Pumpkin**	183°F for 45 to 60 Min (83.9°C)
Brussels Sprouts	183°F for 45 to 60 Min (83.9°C)		**Radish**	183°F for 10 to 25 Min (83.9°C)
Butternut Squash	183°F for 1 to 2 Hours (83.9°C)		**Rhubarb**	141°F for 25 to 45 Min (60.6°C)
Cabbage	183°F for 30 to 45 Min (83.9°C)		**Rutabaga**	183°F for 2 Hours (83.9°C)
Carrot	183°F for 40 to 60 Min (83.9°C)		**Salsify**	183°F for 45 to 60 Min (83.9°C)
Cauliflower			**Squash, Summer**	183°F for 30 to 60 Min (83.9°C)
Florets	183°F for 20 to 30 Min (83.9°C)		**Squash, Winter**	183°F for 1 to 2 Hours (83.9°C)
For Puree	183°F for 2 Hours (83.9°C)		**Sunchokes**	183°F for 40 to 60 Min (83.9°C)
Stems	183°F for 60 to 75 Min (83.9°C)		**Sweet Potatoes**	
Celery Root	183°F for 60 to 75 Min (83.9°C)		Small	183°F for 45 to 60 Min (83.9°C)
Chard	183°F for 60 to 75 Min (83.9°C)		Large	183°F for 60 to 90 Min (83.9°C)
Cherries	183°F for 15 to 25 Min (83.9°C)		**Swiss Chard**	183°F for 60 to 75 Min (83.9°C)
Corn	183°F for 30 to 45 Min (83.9°C)		**Turnip**	183°F for 30 to 45 Min (83.9°C)
Eggplant	183°F for 30 to 45 Min (83.9°C)		**Yams**	183°F for 30 to 60 Min (83.9°C)
Fennel	183°F for 40 to 60 Min (83.9°C)		**Zucchini**	183°F for 30 to 60 Min (83.9°C)
Golden Beets	183°F for 30 to 60 Min (83.9°C)			
Green Beans	183°F for 30 to 45 Min (83.9°C)			
Leek	183°F for 30 to 60 Min (83.9°C)			
Onion	183°F for 35 to 45 Min (83.9°C)			
Parsnip	183°F for 30 to 60 Min (83.9°C)			
Pea Pods	183°F for 30 to 40 Min (83.9°C)			
Peaches	183°F for 30 to 60 Min (83.9°C)			

Lamb

Arm Chop

Medium Rare	131°F for 18 to 36 Hours (55.0°C)
Medium	140°F for 18 to 36 Hours (60.0°C)

Blade Chop

Medium Rare	131°F for 18 to 36 Hours (55.0°C)
Medium	140°F for 18 to 36 Hours (60.0°C)

Breast

Medium-Rare	131°F for 20 to 28 Hours (55.0°C)
Medium	140°F for 20 to 28 Hours (60.0°C)
Well-Traditional	165°F for 20 to 28 Hours (73.9°C)

Leg, Bone In

Rare	126°F for 1 to 2 Days (52.2°C)
Medium Rare	131°F for 2 to 3 Days (55.0°C)
Medium	140°F for 1 to 3 Days (60.0°C)

Leg, Boneless

Medium Rare	131°F for 18 to 36 Hours (55.0°C)
Medium	140°F for 18 to 36 Hours (60.0°C)

Loin Chops

Rare	126°F for 1 to 2 Hours (52.2°C)
Medium Rare	131°F for 2 to 4 Hours (55.0°C)
Medium	140°F for 2 to 3 Hours (60.0°C)

Loin Roast

Rare	126°F for 1 to 2 Hours (52.2°C)
Medium Rare	131°F for 2 to 4 Hours (55.0°C)
Medium	140°F for 2 to 3 Hours (60.0°C)

Loin, Boneless

Rare	126°F for 1 to 2 Hours (52.2°C)
Medium Rare	131°F for 2 to 4 Hours (55.0°C)
Medium	140°F for 2 to 3 Hours (60.0°C)

Neck

Medium Rare	131°F for 2 to 3 Days (55.0°C)
Medium	140°F for 2 to 3 Days (60.0°C)
Well-Traditional	165°F for 1 to 2 Days (73.9°C)

Osso Buco

Medium-Rare	131°F for 1 to 2 Days (55.0°C)
Medium	140°F for 1 to 2 Days (60.0°C)
Well-Traditional	165°F for 1 to 2 Days (73.9°C)

Rack

Rare	126°F for 1 to 2 Hours (52.2°C)
Medium Rare	131°F for 2 to 3 Hours (55.0°C)
Medium	140°F for 1 to 3 Hours (60.0°C)

Rib Chop

Rare	126°F for 1 to 2 Hours (52.2°C)
Medium Rare	131°F for 2 to 3 Hours (55.0°C)
Medium	140°F for 1 to 3 Hours (60.0°C)

Ribs

Medium Rare	131°F for 22 to 26 Hours (55.0°C)
Medium	140°F for 22 to 26 Hours (60.0°C)
Well-Traditional	165°F for 22 to 26 Hours (73.9°C)

Shank

Medium Rare	131°F for 1 to 2 Days (55.0°C)
Medium	140°F for 1 to 2 Days (60.0°C)
Well-Traditional	165°F for 1 to 2 Days (73.9°C)

Shoulder

Medium Rare	131°F for 1 to 2 Days (55.0°C)
Medium	140°F for 1 to 2 Days (60.0°C)
Well-Traditional	165°F for 18 to 36 Hours (73.9°C)

Tenderloin

Rare	126°F for 1 to 2 Hours (52.2°C)
Medium Rare	131°F for 2 to 3 Hours (55.0°C)
Medium	140°F for 1 to 3 Hours (60.0°C)

Pork

Arm Steak
Medium Rare   131°F for 1 to 2 Days (55.0°C)
Medium   140°F for 1 to 2 Days (60.0°C)

Baby Back Ribs
Medium Rare   131°F for 8 to 10 Hours (55.0°C)
Medium   140°F for 8 to 10 Hours (60.0°C)
Well-Traditional155°F for 12 to 24 Hours (68.3°C)

Back Ribs
Medium Rare   131°F for 8 to 12 Hours (55.0°C)
Medium   140°F for 8 to 12 Hours (60.0°C)
Well-Traditional155°F for 12 to 24 Hours (68.3°C)

Belly
Low and Slow 140°F for 2 to 3 Days (60.0°C)
In Between   160°F for 18 to 36 Hours (71.1°C)
High and Fast 180°F for 12 to 18 Hours (82.2°C)

Blade Chops
Medium Rare   131°F for 8 to 12 Hours (55.0°C)
Medium   140°F for 8 to 12 Hours (60.0°C)

Blade Roast
Medium Rare   131°F for 1 to 2 Days (55.0°C)
Medium   140°F for 1 to 2 Days (60.0°C)
Well-Traditional155°F for 1 to 2 Days (68.3°C)

Blade Steak
Medium Rare   131°F for 18 to 36 Hours (55.0°C)
Medium   140°F for 18 to 36 Hours (60.0°C)

Boston Butt
Medium Rare   131°F for 1 to 2 Days (55.0°C)
Medium   140°F for 1 to 2 Days (60.0°C)
Well-Traditional155°F for 1 to 2 Days (68.3°C)

Butt Roast
Medium Rare   131°F for 18 to 36 Hours (55.0°C)
Medium   140°F for 18 to 36 Hours (60.0°C)
Well-Traditional155°F for 18 to 36 Hours (68.3°C)

Country Style Ribs
Medium Rare   131°F for 8 to 12 Hours (55.0°C)
Medium   140°F for 8 to 12 Hours (60.0°C)
Well-Traditional155°F for 12 to 24 Hours (68.3°C)

Fresh Side Pork
Low and Slow 140°F for 2 to 3 Days (60.0°C)
In Between   160°F for 18 to 36 Hours (71.1°C)
High and Fast 180°F for 12 to 18 Hours (82.2°C)

Ground Pork
Medium Rare   131°F for 2 to 4 Hours (55.0°C)
Medium   140°F for 2 to 4 Hours (60.0°C)

Ham Roast
Medium Rare   131°F for 10 to 20 Hours (55.0°C)
Medium   140°F for 10 to 20 Hours (60.0°C)
Well-Traditional155°F for 10 to 20 Hours (68.3°C)

Ham Steak
Medium Rare   131°F for 2 to 3 Hours (55.0°C)
Medium   140°F for 2 to 3 Hours (60.0°C)

Kabobs
Medium Rare   131°F for 3 to 8 Hours (55.0°C)
Medium   140°F for 3 to 8 Hours (60.0°C)
Well-Traditional155°F for 3 to 8 Hours (68.3°C)

Leg (Fresh Ham)
Medium Rare   131°F for 10 to 20 Hours (55.0°C)
Medium   140°F for 10 to 20 Hours (60.0°C)
Well-Traditional155°F for 10 to 20 Hours (68.3°C)

Loin Chop
Medium Rare   131°F for 3 to 5 Hours (55.0°C)
Medium   140°F for 2 to 4 Hours (60.0°C)

Loin Roast
Medium Rare   131°F for 4 to 8 Hours (55.0°C)
Medium   140°F for 4 to 6 Hours (60.0°C)

Picnic Roast
Medium Rare   131°F for 1 to 3 Days (55.0°C)
Medium   140°F for 1 to 3 Days (60.0°C)
Well-Traditional155°F for 1 to 3 Days (68.3°C)

Pork Chops
Medium Rare   131°F for 3 to 6 Hours (55.0°C)
Medium   140°F for 2 to 4 Hours (60.0°C)

Rib Chops
Medium Rare   131°F for 5 to 8 Hours (55.0°C)
Medium   140°F for 4 to 7 Hours (60.0°C)

Rib Roast
Medium Rare   131°F for 5 to 8 Hours (55.0°C)
Medium   140°F for 4 to 7 Hours (60.0°C)

Sausage
Medium Rare   131°F for 2 to 3 Hours (55.0°C)
Medium   140°F for 2 to 3 Hours (60.0°C)
Well-Traditional 155°F for 2 to 3 Hours (68.3°C)

Shank
Medium Rare   131°F for 8 to 10 Hours (55.0°C)
Medium   140°F for 8 to 10 Hours (60.0°C)

Shoulder
Medium Rare   135°F for 1 to 2 Days (57.2°C)
Medium   145°F for 1 to 2 Days (62.8°C)
Well-Traditional 155°F for 1 to 2 Days (68.3°C)

Sirloin Chops
Medium Rare   131°F for 6 to 12 Hours (55.0°C)
Medium   140°F for 5 to 10 Hours (60.0°C)

Sirloin Roast
Medium Rare   131°F for 6 to 12 Hours (55.0°C)
Medium   140°F for 5 to 10 Hours (60.0°C)
Well-Traditional 155°F for 10 to 16 Hours (68.3°C)

Spare Ribs
Medium Rare   131°F for 12 to 24 Hours (55.0°C)
Medium   140°F for 12 to 24 Hours (60.0°C)
Well-Traditional 155°F for 12 to 24 Hours (68.3°C)

Spleen
Spleen   145°F for 1 Hour (62.8°C)

Tenderloin
Medium Rare   131°F for 3 to 6 Hours (55.0°C)
Medium   140°F for 2 to 4 Hours (60.0°C)

Turkey

Breast

"Rare"	136°F for 1 to 4 Hours (57.8°C)
Medium - Typical	147°F for 1 to 4 Hours (63.9°C)

Drumstick

Medium-Rare	140°F for 3 to 4 Hours (60.0°C)
Ideal	148°F for 4 to 8 Hours (64.4°C)
For Shredding	160°F for 18 to 24 Hours (71.1°C)

Leg

Medium-Rare	140°F for 3 to 4 Hours (60.0°C)
Ideal	148°F for 4 to 8 Hours (64.4°C)
For Shredding	160°F for 18 to 24 Hours (71.1°C)

Sausage

White Meat	140°F for 1 to 4 Hours (63.9°C)
Mixed Meat	140°F for 3 to 4 Hours (64.4°C)

Thigh

Medium-Rare	140°F for 3 to 4 Hours (60.0°C)
Ideal	148°F for 4 to 8 Hours (64.4°C)
For Shredding	160°F for 18 to 24 Hours (71.1°C)

Fahrenheit to Celsius Conversion

All temperatures in this guide are given in Fahrenheit, however some sous vide equipment only works in Celsius. To convert from Fahrenheit to Celsius take the temperature, then subtract 32 from it and multiply the result by 5/9:

(Fahrenheit - 32) * 5/9 = Celsius

We've listed out the temperatures from 37°C to 87°C which are the most commonly used range in sous vide.

Celsius	Fahrenheit		Celsius	Fahrenheit
37	98.6		64	147.2
38	100.4		65	149.0
39	102.2		66	150.8
40	104.0		67	152.6
41	105.8		68	154.4
42	107.6		69	156.2
43	109.4		70	158.0
44	111.2		71	159.8
45	113.0		72	161.6
46	114.8		73	163.4
47	116.6		74	165.2
48	118.4		75	167.0
49	120.2		76	168.8
50	122.0		77	170.6
51	123.8		78	172.4
52	125.6		79	174.2
53	127.4		80	176.0
54	129.2		81	177.8
55	131.0		82	179.6
56	132.8		83	181.4
57	134.6		84	183.2
58	136.4		85	185.0
59	138.2		86	186.8
60	140.0		87	188.6
61	141.8		88	190.4
62	143.6		89	192.2
63	145.4		90	194.0

Sous Vide Resources

Sous vide is a very complex process and there is much more to learn about it besides what has been covered in this book. There is more and more good information available about sous vide cooking. Here are some resources to help you continue to learn more.

For an up to date look at current books, websites, and other sous vide resources you can visit the list we keep on our website.

You can find it at:
www.cookingsousvide.com/info/sous-vide-resources

Books

Under Pressure

By Thomas Keller

This book shows you the extent of what is possible through sous vide cooking. The recipes aren't easy, and they require a lot of work but they can provide great inspiration for dishes of your own. If you are interested in expanding your concept of what can be accomplished through cooking then this is a must have.

Cooking for Geeks

By Jeff Potter

If you are interested in the Geekier aspects of cooking then this book does a great job. It takes you through the basics of setting up your kitchen all the way up to kitchen hacks and sous vide cooking.

On Food and Cooking

By Harold McGee

This is the ultimate guide to the scientific aspects of cooking. If you like to know why things happen in the kitchen, at every level, you'll find this book fascinating.

Cooking Sous Vide: A Guide for the Home Cook

By Jason Logsdon

My first book and the first book written exclusively for the home cook learning sous vide. Most of the information from it has been updated and adapted for inclusion in this book.

Sous-Vide Cuisine

By Joan Roca

From the authors: "we propose our book, as a progression that involves three concepts of sous-vide: Storage, Cooking and Cuisine." Be sure to get a copy that is in English, as many copies are not.

Modernist Cuisine: The Art and Science of Cooking

By Nathan Myhrvold

This isn't out at the time of publishing but it aims to be the bible of modernist cuisine. It's over 2,400 pages costs $500 and was several years in the making. If you are serious about learning the newly developing modernist techniques then this might be worth the investment.

Sous Vide for the Home Cook

By Douglas Baldwin

Baldwin helped to define and codify home sous vide cooking with his free online guide. His book is a nice intro to the subject, including food safety, and has many simple recipes to follow.

Sous Vide

By Viktor Stampfer

A collection of some of Viktor's best sous vide recipes. Be sure to get a copy that is in English, as many copies are not.

Websites

Cooking Sous Vide

http://www.cookingsousvide.com

This is the main website where I contribute sous vide articles. We update it regularly with original recipes and news from around the sous vide community. There are also community features such as forums and question and answer pages.

SVKitchen

http://www.svkitchen.com

A very nice site on sous vide cooking. They touch on everything from standard sous vide swordfish to making your own preserved lemons with sous vide. The recipes for *Garlic Confit* and *Vanilla Poached Pears* are from their site.

Sous Vide: Recipes, Techniques & Equipment

http://forums.egullet.org/index.php?showtopic=116617&st=0

A very long forum string from eGullet, about 98 pages long at this time that covers almost everything you need to know about sous vide if you have the time to look through it all. I suggest starting near the end and working towards the front.

Apps

We have an iPhone and iPad app available, as well as one coming shortly for the Android. You can search in the app store for "Sous Vide" and ours should be near the top, published by "Primolicious".

PolyScience is also releasing an app in conjunction with us that should be in the app store by the end of the year.

Papers and Research

USDA Guide

http://www.fsis.usda.gov/OPPDE/rdad/FSISNotices/RTE_Poultry_Tables.pdf

The US government guide to poultry and beef cooking times.

Practical Guide to Sous Vide

http://amath.colorado.edu/~baldwind/sous-vide.html

Written by Douglas Baldwin, this is one of the best guides available for the scientific principles behind sous vide cooking and a pioneering work in home sous vide cooking.

Sous Vide Safety

http://www.seriouseats.com/2010/04/sous-vide-basics-low-temperature-chicken.html

A nice look at the basics of low temperature cooking, specifically as it applies to chicken.

Acknowledgments

Sous vide is a relatively new field for the home cook and the effort of several people has been instrumental in moving it forward. Nathan Myhrvold helped to almost single-handedly push sous vide cooking to home cooks through his research and contributions to the eGullet thread as well as his interviews in the mainstream press. Douglas Baldwin wrote his incomparable guide to the science behind sous vide and the research he's done around it. Several manufacturers have been developing sous vide products specifically for the home chef and trying to educate people about the benefits of using sous vide cooking at home. There are also many home cooks out there contributing to the sous vide community through their personal blogs sharing recipes, successes and failures in sous vide. Also, the professional chefs who have been using and perfecting this technique for the last three decades including Thomas Keller, Viktor Stampfer, and Joan Roca.

This book would not have been possible without all of their hard work and the information they have made available to the community.

And finally, thanks to my parents and my wife for encouraging me in everything I do. I would never have been able to do any of this without their support.

About the Author

Jason Logsdon is an avid cook and web developer. He is a co-founder of and main contributor to CookingSousVide.com. He can be reached at jason@cookingsousvide.com.

End Notes

[1] For more information about heat and it's effects on meat I suggest *On Food and Cooking* by Harold McGee, it has about all the food science information you could ever want.

[2] You can find the USDA guide here:
http://www.fsis.usda.gov/OPPDE/rdad/FSISNotices/RTE_Poultry_Tables.pdf

[3] *A Practical Guide to Sous Vide* was one of the pioneering works on sous vide and can be found here:
http://amath.colorado.edu/~baldwind/sous-vide.html

[4] Serious Eats has a very good look at the safety of chicken in regards to temperature here:
http://www.seriouseats.com/2010/04/sous-vide-basics-low-temperature-chicken.html

[5] This is also the finding of the French Culinary Institute and expressed in their Sous Vide Primer:
http://www.cookingissues.com/2010/04/07/sous-vide-and-low-temp-primer-part-ii-cooking-without-a-vacuum/

[6] I personally use a FoodSaver and have had pretty good success with it though I also use Ziplocs very often when I'm in a rush or don't feel like pulling out the FoodSaver. Some models of the FoodSaver work better than others and I recommend doing some research on Amazon and reading the ratings and reviews there.

[7] I have worked professionally with PolyScience and use one of their circulators at home that they have loaned to me. It's worth looking at other options if you feel my opinion has been compromised.

[8] The Seattle Food Geek has many great articles if you are interested in the more nerdy and science-y side of cooking.
http://seattlefoodgeek.com/2010/02/diy-sous-vide-heating-immersion-circulator-for-about-75

[9] Again, I've worked with PolyScience before, feel free to look at other brands if you feel I am biased.

[10] I've also used a demo version of the Sous Vide Supreme that they loaned to me. It was very good and cooked most dishes adequately. They also have very good customer service.

[11] I regularly used a SousVideMagic controller with an old crock pot until PolyScience loaned me their circulator. The SousVideMagic worked very well, especially for the price. They also have great customer service.

[12] You can read the article and the following discussion here:
http://www.seriouseats.com/2010/04/cook-your-meat-in-a-beer-cooler-the-worlds-best-sous-vide-hack.html

[13] Looking up the FoodSavers on Amazon and reading the reviews can be a great way to get a feel for how the different models respond.

[14] Once again, I've worked with PolyScience before so feel free to look at other brands if you feel my opinion has been compromised.

[15] Again, I've also used a demo version of the Sous Vide Supreme that they loaned to me.

[16] Here's the link to that article again:
http://www.seriouseats.com/2010/04/cook-your-meat-in-a-beer-cooler-the-worlds-best-sous-vide-hack.html

[17] To find farmers markets in your area you can check out the following links:
http://www.localharvest.org/
http://apps.ams.usda.gov/FarmersMarkets/
http://www.ams.usda.gov/AMSv1.0/FARMERSMARKETS

[18] The one I use was loaned out to me from PolyScience, you can find it here:
http://www.cuisinetechnology.com/the-smoking-gun.php

[19] Serious Eats did some studies that show that people in a blind taste test prefer medium-rare steak, even if they state they usually prefer rare or medium steaks.
http://www.seriouseats.com/2010/03/how-to-sous-vide-steak.html

[20] If you are at all interested in smoking, curing, sausage making, or any of the other forms of charcuterie then Michael Ruhlman's Charcuterie is a must have book. It makes the process simple and approachable. You can find it at Amazon here:
http://www.amazon.com/Charcuterie-Craft-Salting-Smoking-Curing/dp/0393058298/

[21] Michael Ruhlman's blog is one of the only "must read" food blogs I have. You can find it here:
http://ruhlman.com/

[22] You can find vanilla paste online, such as at Williams-Sonoma:
http://www.williams-sonoma.com/products/2749604/

10412964R0

Made in the USA
Lexington, KY
21 July 2011